States of Emergency in Liberal Democracies

In an emergency, statesmen concentrate power and suspend citizens' rights. These emergency powers are ubiquitous in the crisis government of liberal democracies, but their nature and justification are poorly understood. Based on a pluralist conception of political ethics and political power, this book shows how we can avoid the dangers and confusions inherent in the norm/exception approach that dominates both historical and contemporary debate. The book shows how liberal values need never – indeed must never – be suspended, even in times of urgency. Only then can accountability remain a live possibility. But at the same time, emergency powers can sometimes be justified with reference to extra-liberal norms that also operate in times of normalcy. By emphasizing the continuity between times of normalcy and emergency, the book illuminates the norms of crisis government, broadening our understanding of liberal democratic government and of political ethics in the process.

Nomi Claire Lazar is currently the Canadian Bicentennial Visiting Fellow at Yale University. From 2005 to 2008, she held the position of Collegiate Assistant Professor and Harper-Schmidt Fellow at the University of Chicago. She holds a Ph.D. in political science from Yale University and degrees in philosophy from the University of Toronto and in legal and political theory from the School of Public Policy, University College, London. Prior to returning to graduate school, she worked in the Criminal Law Policy section of the Canadian Justice Department. Her writing has appeared in the journals *Politics and Society*, *Constellations*, and *Political Theory* and will soon appear in the *University of Toronto Law Journal*.

States of Emergency in Liberal Democracies

NOMI CLAIRE LAZAR

Yale University

CAMBRIDGE UNIVERSITY PRESS

Cambridge, New York, Melbourne, Madrid, Cape Town, Singapore, São Paulo, Delhi

Cambridge University Press
32 Avenue of the Americas, New York, NY 10013-2473, USA

www.cambridge.org
Information on this title: www.cambridge.org/9780521449694

First published 2009

Printed in the United States of America

A catalog record for this publication is available from the British Library.

Library of Congress Cataloging in Publication Data

Lazar, Nomi Claire, 1975–
States of emergency in liberal democracies / Nomi Claire Lazar.
    p. cm.
Includes bibliographical references and index.
ISBN 978-0-521-44969-4 (hardback)
1. War and emergency powers. 2. Democracy. 3. Liberalism. 4. Rule of law. I. Title.

JF256.L39 2009
323.4′9–dc22   2008048942

ISBN 978-0-521-44969-4 hardback

Contents

Acknowledgments

I am grateful to have had the opportunity to discuss the material in this book before a number of audiences and with a number of colleagues and teachers.

I wish to acknowledge Seyla Benhabib, Lynd Forguson, John P. McCormick, Fred Rosen, Frances Rosenbluth, and Ian Shapiro for their intellectual guidance, encouragement, and support, some with this project and some in the years leading up to it. Most of all, Steven Smith, who supervised the dissertation from which this book grew, deserves a true debt of gratitude for allowing me to rove freely and what must sometimes have appeared randomly, while always asking just the right question at just the right juncture to make me think a little deeper or push a little further. He is a teacher in the finest and truest sense. Patchen Markell and the late Iris Marion Young both provided sound advice at the end of the process. Along the way, conversations with Melvin Rogers, H. Abbie Erler, Jennifer Tobin, Mayling Birney, and Timothy Pachirat were always fun and inspiring.

When presenting ideas from this work at meetings of the American Political Science Association and the Canadian Political Science Association and at the University of Chicago, the National University of Singapore, the New School, the University of Southern Mississippi, and Yale, I benefited greatly from the insight and suggestions of a number of people. In particular, I am indebted to Bruce Ackerman, David Dyzenhaus, Oren Gross, Sanford Levinson, Victor V. Ramraj, Kent Roach,

Bill Scheuerman, Mark Tushnet, and several anonymous reviewers for lively exchanges and helpful feedback.

At various stages, I have been grateful for the financial support of the Social Sciences and Humanities Research Council of Canada, Yale University, and the H. B. Earhart Foundation.

A previous version of Chapter 2 appeared in *Politics and Society* in June 2005 as "Must Exceptionalism Prove the Rule?" and I am grateful to Sage Publications for allowing me to include it. Similar thanks are due to Blackwell for the use of Chapter 5, "The Rule of Law and the Roman Dictatorship," a previous version of which appeared in *Constellations* in December 2006.

My parents, Frum and Alex Himelfarb and Avrim Lazar and his wife Valerie Clements, the ever energizing Mildred Lazar, and my excellent and constant friend Naomi K. Lewis have all provided warmth, support, and advice. In their various ways, they have influenced this book, sometimes profoundly. This book is dedicated to my dear husband, Emanuel, and to the memory of our sons, Isaac and Samuel.

States of Emergency in Liberal Democracies

I

The Problem of Emergency

Tensions between order and justice are inherent in any constitutional regime. Order requires constraint and justice suggests rights and freedoms. While the everyday struggles between these two values often escape our notice, they clash spectacularly in times of emergency. Nurtured in security and stability, contemporary liberal theory, in the absence of an immediate crisis, has been mostly silent on this subject.[1] Nonetheless most liberal democracies[2] have standing constitutional or

---

[1] There are two classic studies of the related concept of reason of state in the history of political thought: C. J. Friederich, *Constitutional Reason of State*; and Friederich Meinecke, *Machiavellism: The Doctrine of Raison D'état and Its Place in Modern History*. Also, there is a voluminous legal literature on emergency rights derogations that includes Jaime Oraà, *Human Rights in States of Emergency in International Law*; Anna-Lena Svensson-McCarthy, *International Law of Human Rights and States of Exception*; Christoph Schreuer, "Derogation of Human Rights in Situations of Public Emergency: The Experience of the European Convention on Human Rights"; Allan Rosas, "Emergency Regimes: A Comparison"; and M. Radin, "Martial Law and the State of Siege." More recent work, primarily among legal scholars, has included Bruce Ackerman, *Before the Next Attack: Preserving Civil Liberties in an Age of Terrorism*; David Dyzenhaus, *The Constitution of Law: Legality in a Time of Emergency*; and Oren Gross and Fionnuala Ní Aoláin, *Law in Times of Crisis: Emergency Powers in Theory and Practice*.

[2] For the purposes of this book, a liberal democracy is a state that meets criteria, loosely adapted from J. Denis Derbyshire and Ian Derbyshire, *Political Systems of the World*, p. 29, as follows: 1) Regular free elections of candidates from multiple parties to representative institutions; 2) limited government; 3) an independent judiciary that guarantees core rights connected with human dignity such as freedom of assembly, freedom of expression, and due process of law.

special legal powers to derogate rights and the rule of law for the sake of order in times of crisis; and when a crisis arises, those states that do not have such powers use impromptu ones anyway. This is no ivory tower puzzle, and these powers are exercised more often than we think.[3] This book aims to help theory touch its feet to the ground.

Given that liberal democracy is essentially bound up with the division of powers and the preservation of rights and freedoms, how could emergency powers, which impose order through constraint of these features, *ever* be justly constituted and exercised? How can liberal democratic values accommodate powers or institutions that seem inherently illiberal? And, given that emergencies are common and often unpredictable, how can a liberal democratic state survive without them? On the one hand, in resorting to such powers the state ceases to be liberal, while on the other, in not resorting to them, the state might well cease to be.[4] At a minimum, failing to effectively confront a crisis results in a significant loss of life and property. The dilemma is an old one. It is a concrete manifestation of the tensions between order and justice, between the enablement and constraint of power, tensions that are inherent in any constitutional regime.

While contemporary neo-Kantian philosophical liberalism lacks sufficient resources from which to draw argument or inspiration for confronting this puzzle, many absolutists make the problem central to their conceptions of politics, and hence set the terms of the debate. Carl Schmitt in particular dominates the field of emergency powers, and his

---

[3] Two recent examples are the flooding of New Orleans and the riots in France. President Bush declared a state of emergency for the state of Louisiana on August 27, 2005. The French Government also declared a state of emergency, on November 9, 2005. Bangladesh was under a state of emergency in January 2007. And these are just a small handful of examples. Indeed, there was a de facto or de jure state of emergency declared in more than 90 countries between 1985 and 1995, including such strong Western democracies as France, the United Kingdom, Canada, and the United States. See United Nations Commission on Human Rights, *Eighth Annual Report and List of States which, since 1 January 1985 Have Proclaimed, Extended, or Terminated a State of Emergency.*

[4] Ronald Dworkin characterizes the problem in a similar way in his article "Terror and the Attack on Civil Liberties."

legacy is the assimilation of emergency to the exception and suspension of rules and norms.[5] This is evident, for instance, in the current fashion for Giorgio Agamben, whose work, despite himself, is fundamentally Schmittian. Overwhelmingly, emergencies and emergency powers are treated with reference to this dichotomy between norms and exceptions, which John Ferejohn and Pasquale Pasquino have called "the structure of emergency powers."[6] The exceptionalist view is that norms apply only in normal situations; in a real crisis, emergency powers do not violate rights and the rule of law because these rules are simply not in effect at such exceptional times. Emergency powers are thus amoral and beyond the usual norms: one cannot violate a rule that is not in effect. Carl Schmitt is an amoralist about emergency powers, but so, arguably, are Richard Posner and former U.S. Chief Justice William Rehnquist.[7] In arguing that we cannot make exceptions from moral *or* legal norms, even liberals who hold emergency powers to be unjust speak in these terms. William Scheuerman argues that "the rule of law was designed for bad times as well as good ones," and Michael Ignatieff has worried that "If laws are rules, and emergencies make exceptions to these rules, how can their authority survive once exceptions are made?"[8] David Dyzenhaus argues that law that compromises is necessarily not only morally but legally compromised. Law cannot be law if it makes room for exceptions.[9] Emergency powers are immoral if making exceptions to laws and moral rules is always immoral. Franz Neumann has claimed that emergency powers allow the state to "annihilate civil liberties altogether."[10] And Jules Lobel has argued, from the American case, that the problem of exceptions has meant that liberals – among whom we might perhaps

---

[5] It is true that emergencies were understood as 'exceptions' before Schmitt. Constitutions sometimes term special powers '*pouvoirs exceptionels*' or speak of an '*Ausnahmezustand*' – an exceptional situation. But it is Schmitt's particular language that has been assimilated into most contemporary legal and theoretical discussions.

[6] John Ferejohn and Pasquale Pasquino, "The Law of Exception: A Typology of Emergency Powers," p. 221. See also Philip B. Heymann, *Terrorism, Freedom, and Security: Winning without War*, xii.

[7] Richard Posner, *Not a Suicide Pact*, p. 12. William H. Rehnquist, *All the Laws but One*.

[8] William Scheuerman, "Rethinking Crisis Government," p. 492. Michael Ignatieff, *The Lesser Evil: Political Ethics in an Age of Terror*, p. 25. See also Giorgio Agamben, *State of Exception*.

[9] Dyzenhaus, *The Constitution of Law*, e.g., p. 7.

[10] Franz Neumann, "The Concept of Political Freedom," p. 917.

count Oren Gross – have aimed to "separate emergency rule from the normal constitutional order, thereby preserving the Constitution in its pristine form."[11] Both those who claim that emergency powers are amoral and those who claim that they are immoral rely on a dichotomy between norms and exceptions, whether those norms are legal-institutional, moral, or descriptive. One aim of this book, then, is to escape from this essentially Schmittian conceptual framework in both its left and right permutations.

I argue that a theoretical framework for thinking about emergencies grounded in the norm/exception dichotomy is empirically and ethically suspect. This is true regardless of whether one accepts or rejects exceptions to norms. And this is not just a matter for abstract concern: those who embrace the exception as a discrete category in the first place provide a carte blanche for politicians. If norms are suspended, anything goes. Under cover of emergency and armed with such a license, statesmen have gone well beyond what is strictly necessary to cope with an emergency in order to reach ends that are themselves unnecessary or even abhorrent. But if we accept the norm/exception dichotomy and reject the license that the idea of *exception* provides, the remaining option is to join with those who hold that emergency powers are not justifiable. This view is self-defeating. Justice and order are inextricable. And because threats to order, and hence to justice, are real, it follows that, to the extent that we value the protection of human rights and the rule of law, we cannot ignore the exigencies that emergency presents. At the extreme, destruction of the state would mean the destruction of justice and liberal values too, and states have a responsibility to work to protect their citizens from serious harm.

In developing an alternative conceptual framework, I aim specifically to undermine the norm/exception perspective in order to show how emergency powers might be exercised while liberal norms remain in force. I argue that understanding emergency powers in terms of their continuities with everyday institutions and values is more accurate both descriptively and normatively. It helps us to see how such powers could *ever* be justified, and it points to directions for making them a little safer. If our eyes are opened by what I will call 'an ethics of experience' to descriptive, moral, and institutional continuities, we can

---

[11] Jules Lobel, "Emergency Power and the Decline of Liberalism," p. 1390.

see that, under states of emergency, normal ethics do not cease to function. There is no exception; rights do not lose their force, and the values underlying the rule of law do not lose their power. Political leaders may be held to the same standards of moral and institutional accountability to which they are always held in executing their duties.

Emergency powers are justified – when they are justified – because they embody principles that already function under normal circumstances. Order is a value also, and it animates the day-to-day life of the state alongside liberal values, for instance in the workings of the criminal justice system, which every liberal democratic state requires. Rights are derogated for the sake of order every day.

Emergency provisions that concentrate power also show salient continuities. To the extent that the rule of law is instrumental to more fundamental values, and to the extent that a shift in formal and informal power and constraint does not preclude furthering those values, mitigating the rule of law is not *exceptional*. So long as emergency powers are well designed and exercised within the limits of international law, they need no *special* justification. Elements of urgency and scale cause a shift in the relationship between principles of justice and principles of order, and between formal and informal constraints on power. But this is a shift and not a sea change. Normal and emergency values are continuous. Normal and exceptional institutions have important elements of continuity also. By decentering the norm/exception dichotomy, we can see how liberal democracies might remain such, even as they derogate rights and the rule of law.

My arguments have several practical and theoretical implications. Practically, a clearer understanding of the ethics of emergency can illuminate debates about emergency institutions and their use in particular cases. Ideally, clarity would reduce the potential for dangerous rhetoric and executive excess. Emergencies are inherently dangerous regardless, but throughout the book, I present principles instrumental in improving safety.

Theoretical implications are many. First, the arguments in the chapters that follow provide an answer to Carl Schmitt's charge that liberal parliamentary government is incapable of addressing "the exception." I call into question a number of Schmittian claims and conceptual categories, including his understanding of sovereignty and of dictatorship, and I show how the Schmittian problem of "the exception" can be avoided by removing emergency from its purview.

Second, a study of emergency powers has important ramifications for our understanding of liberal theory in general. Emergency illuminates epistemological elements of liberalism as well as liberal conceptual geography. Often, problems at the periphery of theories can illuminate much at the center. Emergency seeds antinomies in a purely rational-deductive political ethics. Hence I will argue that those liberalisms grounded in synthetic a priori principles alone are in trouble. Instead, political ethics must grow from an interaction between rationally grounded principles and those induced from experience. While rational-deductive political ethics may help in establishing moral ends, experience is necessary to understand what might constitute fulfilling those ends and how we might go about doing so. An ethics should help guide our actions and help us in judging the actions of others, and this must remain true even in situations that are incredibly complex, and even in those that are simply squalid. Ultimately, ethics must be elaborated on the ground from a mixture of principles that rest both on abstract axioms and on the experience of concrete application. Stuart Hampshire and Ian Shapiro have pointed out the fairytale-like quality of philosophical work on ethics and politics in recent years, and this book aligns itself with their pragmatic approach.[12] Along these lines I will argue that institutions ought to represent the 'most moral means' to normative ends, a perspective that relies on an understanding of the relationship between deontological and consequentialist conceptions of ethics.

A further ramification concerns the field of application of liberal principles, which, I will argue, are not coextensive with the political ethics that animate liberal democracies in general. Those derogations of civil and political rights that states of emergency allow are justified on the basis of countervailing values related to order. Rights are derogated for the sake of order every day, too. It follows from this that liberal values are not alone in providing moral animation to political life. I will argue for a kind of ethical-political pluralism that obviates the need for the logical gymnastics of some recent philosophical liberals who wish to recognize the value of culture or patriotism.

Before I turn to an overview of the chapters that follow, some elements of my approach, both methodological and conceptual, as well as

---

[12] Stuart Hampshire, *Innocence and Experience*; Ian Shapiro, *The Flight from Reality in the Social Sciences*.

matters of definition deserve attention. The central concept of emergency in particular warrants some clarification. It is important to keep in mind that no set of characteristics *precisely* defines an emergency. There is no exact definition that could be provided that would leave no grey edges. This is widely recognized, and political thinkers have sometimes accused these grey edges of providing room for politicians to abuse emergency powers, a concern that is well founded. But this is not a reason to reject the entire category of emergency, or to fault those whose definitions have proved imprecise. Emergency is among those words that Wittgenstein has taught us to think of as naming not one but a family of concepts, which resemble each other in much the manner that families do.

Just as we can't say precisely what constitutes love or liberty, and just as most diseases are diagnosed by a critical mass of symptoms, rather than by means of a definitive binary determination, the fact that we cannot describe with any precision what constitutes an emergency does not leave us entirely without resources.

What we can do is to describe a family of characteristics that emergencies are likely to display, and when a critical mass of these manifest, people are likely, independently, to come to the conclusion that an emergency is in progress. Of course, some cases will be clearer than others, and, as I argue, those who design institutions would do well to make the calculus favor extra caution when cases are extra ambiguous.

The key characteristics or 'symptoms' of emergencies are urgency and scale. To say that a situation is urgent is to say that it poses an immediate threat, one too pressing to be dealt with through the normal, years-long process of policy and legislation making. An urgent threat is one that must be dealt with immediately, if it is to be eliminated or mitigated. Citizens cannot wait for lengthy bicameral debate to decide on the best way to confront an epidemic, at the risk of allowing the epidemic to spread exponentially, with exponentially greater loss of life.

It is noteworthy that the idea of urgency does not necessarily entail temporal containment. Conceivably, something can remain urgent for a while. A person who is fighting cancer urgently needs medical attention, but that medical attention may be needed on an ongoing basis. The urgency is not just at T_1, as it might be, for instance, with a broken bone. It continues through time until the cancer is cured or in remission.

At the same time, the longer a threat continues, the more opportunity a government has to pass well-considered legislation to deal with new circumstances, or to update existing legislation as the need may be. Hence, time limits on emergency powers make sense.

The second characteristic is what I have called 'scale.' Scale refers to the range of people likely to be affected by the event. A man who has had a heart attack is experiencing an emergency, but it is not an emergency from the perspective of the state. If a power grid disaster shuts down all the hospitals so that he and others cannot receive care, it becomes a matter of emergency for the government, at whatever level of jurisdiction.

While the focus in much recent work has been on terrorist emergencies, there is no principled reason to make an ontological distinction between terrorist threats and other kinds of threats. Infrastructure disasters, epidemics, floods, earthquakes, indeed anything that poses a real and urgent threat on a grand scale is an emergency, insofar as one aspect of a government's job is to keep its citizens safe.

Probably, we would all agree that the tsunami of December, 2004, was an emergency. And, likely, any nation undergoing an invasion is suffering an emergency. Perhaps we'd all agree that a cholera outbreak is an emergency as well. These are clear cases. But what about SARS? What about the Mississippi floods in 2008, or a snowstorm in Connecticut? What scale must an event take on before it can count as an emergency?

This is not a matter that can be laid out with any certainty in advance. What we can do is lay out principles that should be taken into account in emergency declaration and decision making. This is one task of this book. Definition is necessarily political and contested, but that no more removes it from democratic sway than is the case for any other matter of policy or approach. The meaning of equality is equally contested, but no one demands a sovereign decision. Following the naming of an event as an emergency, some form of deliberation and accountability can be engineered.

To prevent misdirection, I want now to turn attention to what I am not arguing. First, I am not arguing that emergency powers can be made completely safe or just. Scholars constantly point to dangers in each other's institutional accounts as a mode of critique. But emergencies are fundamentally dangerous. Even the most genius emergency institutions can be subverted by a cunning and charismatic leader, and the lack of emergency powers has proved no safer. Emergency powers are only more or less safe: a good set of emergency powers is safer than a bad set, and safer still than no emergency powers at all. Hence an effective critique must go beyond a charge of 'unsafe' to outline what is safer.

Second, despite my intention to show that emergency powers might be justifiable, I do not mean to suggest that any particular exercise of emergency powers is justified. Hence, it is no objection to my arguments to point to cases of ill-use. I mean only to show how emergency powers could *ever* be justified. If we can point to even one use of emergency powers that seems justifiable, it makes sense to ask how.

Asking how necessitates clarity about what exactly requires justification. A political ethics of emergency governs both the design of emergency institutions and emergency decision making, and these are not so distinct. The design of institutions, emergency and otherwise, is a normative endeavor, because institutions embody moral values and because institutions contribute to morally relevant outcomes. But institutions are partly made up of offices, and these offices are inhabited by individuals. Because office holders are also individuals, their decisions have a two-fold moral character. For example, when, in the United States, a Governor decides whether to grant a pardon to a condemned person, he or she is responsible for that person's life both as an individual human being with the same moral duties as any other person, and as a political leader who has taken on certain official responsibilities, including the duties to uphold and execute the law. For our purposes, it is primarily the official aspect of ethical-political decision making that is salient. In politics generally, and in times of emergency particularly, decision making is itself an institution, and the decisions of office holders have an institutional character.

We often think of institutions as largely constituted by rules. But while politics might, to a great extent, be rule governed, it is not rule determined. Office holders are agents and the agency they exercise is on our behalf. Just as we might send an agent to conduct some business on our behalf with a mandate and a set of limitations only, our political representatives are not automatons. Their agency is of a creative and interpretive variety. They exercise judgment. And this is not an externality. Most offices are explicitly designed for agents and the agency of an office holder is itself part of the institution; it is an element – indeed a core element – of the office itself.

Hence, when we speak about whether it is right to do wrong with respect to emergency rights derogations, and when we consider how emergency powers might be justified, we should recognize that these are *both* institutional questions, because the office holder's capacity to make decisions on political matters is itself an institutional function. Whether the existence of emergency powers can be justified and whether an office holder is ever justified in using them are, though not the same question, at least intrinsically related. Having emergency powers in the first place assumes the agency of the office holder.

In a similar vein, I want to underline the salient similarities between varieties of legal and moral rights for the purposes of the arguments that follow. Many theorists stress exception from *either* legal or moral norms, while others stress myriad varieties of interconnectedness between the two. Here the two are connected with respect to modes of justification. Sometimes, a declaration of emergency is necessary not because constitutionally enshrined civil rights prevent certain actions, but rather because the activities instigated under the declaration of martial law violate the moral rights of colonial denizens, enshrined in the common law, rather than in a constitution. There are *both* moral and legal prohibitions against killing people and torching their houses, even where there is no constitutional sanctification of life and property. I do not mean to suggest that all these kinds of violations – constitutional, legal, and moral – are interchangeable. However, for the purposes of the problem under investigation, their differences are less important than their similarities. Whatever justification we might find for the derogation of one kind of right could serve as justification for the others also.

The core of the arguments in this book concern the justice of doing wrong, and there are good reasons for understanding law breaking as wrong both to the extent that, other things being equal, abiding by the law is a moral duty, and because legally enshrined rights share moral content with the same rights outside a state context, even if such rights are not actual. Moral rights are a way of talking about moral claims of particular weight. Enshrining them in legal documents serves both to actualize them by making them enforceable and to signal that the moral claims embodied in those rights constitute fundamental values of the state in question. But the moral information is the same regardless of whether these rights are legislated, constitutional, or moral, actual or potential.

Hence, for our purposes, allowing legal and moral rights to overlap and slip into one another is not so troubling because the concern is with the moral information they contain. Even in practice, the difference between constitutional and legal documents is not always clear-cut. Britain and many of its former colonies, for instance Canada and New Zealand, have diverse foundational documents that are separate from any formal constitution, but still address the issues of procedures and boundaries on government action. In Israel, for instance, where there is no formal constitution, there are laws that are designated as basic. For our current purposes, we need not worry excessively about whether the rights or moral proscriptions in question are formalized in a treaty, in a law, or in a constitution, as rights or otherwise. The important thing is the underlying moral claim regardless of how this claim is manifested.

The final clarification I wish to make concerns the variety of methodologies I employ in approaching the question. The book begins with an account of emergency in the history of political thought, then moves into analytic normative theory and a discussion of historical cases. Some might question the coherence of such an approach. Yet, there are good methodological reasons for beginning a normative investigation with an inquiry into sources in the history of political thought and grounding and illustrating normative argument through historical cases.

First, insofar as institutions grow out of ideas fed through the mill of politics, an inquiry that concerns shifts in institutional structures can benefit from attention to how such shifts were conceived of historically. Second, insofar as political ideas in turn grow out of political life, and are made rigorous through individual brilliance, understanding how the problem of emergency has been formulated and addressed by political thinkers historically can help illuminate its contemporary aspects. In other words, beginning with an examination of the question of emergency in the history of political thought can help us understand the source of contemporary theoretical assumptions about emergency powers as well as contemporary political and institutional actualities. This approach also provides glimpses of possible solutions. The accounts here are intended to give a broad overview of the roots of exceptionalist thinking in the history of political thought, and thus the interpretations I provide are brief sketches.

My use of cases also calls for methodological clarification. Although the cases I discuss raise interesting problems of their own and are suggestive of possible empirical hypotheses that warrant testing, their primary purpose is to serve as illustrations. Thus, the cases are selected according to their illustrative capacity rather than on any more rigorous methodological grounds. While rigorous case studies would be tremendously useful in developing hypotheses for empirical testing, the normative inquiry here is prerequisite. For, before we can ask what would constitute sound emergency powers, we must determine whether emergency powers could ever be sound in the first place. Keeping these caveats and clarifications in mind, here is how I set about exploring these questions.

How did we come to think of emergencies in terms of norms and exceptions? Chapter 2 begins an investigation into the conceptual roots of contemporary perspectives on emergency powers by exploring the exceptionalist strand in the history of political thought. Exceptionalism is the doctrine that the usual norms cease to apply in emergencies. To the question "how could emergency powers in liberal democracies be morally justified?" an exceptionalist would reply, "Emergency powers need no justification because norms apply only to the normal circumstance." If a rule does not apply, we cannot violate it.

I explore exceptionalists of two types: republican and decisionist. Republican exceptionalism is informed by broader ideological aims, in particular, the founding and preservation of a certain kind of state. This view is exemplified in the works of Machiavelli and Rousseau, which exhibit a bifurcated ethics of emergency whose parts I term 'existential' and 'quotidian.' Existential ethics concern the founding and preserving of states while quotidian ethics govern life within a state. Extraordinary statesmen, exempt from quotidian or pedestrian ethics, wield existential ethics. Because emergency is constantly potential, the split between the two kinds of ethics is not temporal. It is not a question of *when* existential ethics should be wielded but of *who* wields them. Exceptional statesmen are always exempt from everyday ethics.

Decisionist exceptionalism finds exemplars in Schmitt and Hobbes. Here, ideological aims (and hence existential ethics) are less central and, instead, the imperatives of what I call 'decisionist logic' come to the fore. Humans are untrustworthy and vicious, nature is still unpredictable: the world is not strictly governed by norms. To respond to such a world under normative restrictions and according to rules would therefore be fundamentally misguided. Deliberation and checks and balances would simply lead to further chaos. Only decisive and absolute sovereignty, entirely unrestricted by earthly norms, can govern here. Like the republican exceptionalists, the decisionists reject the temporal element of emergency powers, the rhetorical illusion that special powers relate to a temporally distinct condition as opposed to a specific person.

Emergency is the permanent condition of humankind, whether potentially or actually, for exceptionalists of both kinds. Their politics and political ethics follow accordingly. Exceptionalists reject the idea that political order is a mechanism that, once set going, runs itself. Instead, this mechanism is flawed. It breaks. It is unpredictable. It may confront objects it was not originally designed to confront, and hence it must be run and maintained by *someone*. Exceptionalism poses a powerful challenge to liberal democratic regimes because it raises the question of whether the law can rule on its own.

To the extent that exceptionalism negates the possibility of accountability by negating moral criteria against which a statesman[13] could be judged, we should be cautious in understanding emergency powers in these terms. Exceptionalism entails, and is entailed by, assumptions that are antithetical to liberal values. We should look to possible alternatives.

Chapter 3 examines the extent to which liberals, historically, have provided such alternatives without succumbing to the norm/exception dichotomy. I argue that neo-Kantian liberalism cannot accommodate emergency powers because it is grounded in a Kantian ethics made up of synthetic a priori moral propositions. Principles that are necessary, because universal, cannot conflict with other principles nor can they be suspended. Exceptions cannot be made nor can countervailing values

[13] In this book, I occasionally use gendered language to refer to political actors. Where I do so, it reflects one of two considerations. Sometimes, as here, our language lacks an appropriate gender-neutral term. Whenever I use 'statesman,' I mean it to refer to either a woman or a man who, as a particular kind of political leader, personifies the state and acts on its authority. The term has a moral component that other terms lack. I have aimed to alternate between referring to such persons as 'he' or 'she.' Where I use 'he' consistently, 'she' would be an anachronism or would be specifically rejected by the thinker in question: as with Rousseau, for whom, based at least on the assessment of women latent in his account of Sophie in *Émile*, the idea of a female political leader could serve only as a joke.

be admitted. As a result, in much of the work of twentieth century canonical liberals, emergency is conspicuous through its absence. Neo-Kantianism draws on Kant's ethics only, largely ignoring his political thought. The chapter's account of Kant's own occasional confrontation with emergency makes this clear.

Neo-Kantian liberals often minimize the role of conflict in politics. They subscribe to a version of Rousseau's perfectibility thesis. This is the claim that humans as they are become humans as they might be under institutions as they might be. In other words, given just institutions, the necessity for enforcement (and also the possibility of emergency) disintegrates. But if one is committed to taking humans as they are, empirically speaking, then neo-Kantian liberalism has little to offer in response to the exceptionalist challenge.

By contrast, Locke's liberalism offers an alternative direction for inquiry by showing how a degree of flexibility can be compatible with liberal institutions. Liberalism need not entail a system of law that rules on its own. Locke may come to many of the same institutional conclusions as other liberals, but he comes to these conclusions in a different way. Instead of deducing them from our inherent nature, or from some higher principle, Locke's arguments begin with the ends of society. And because it is the duty of a statesman to meet those ends, institutional designers must look to empirical information to determine what institutions would be most effective. Locke's arguments for liberal institutions are empirical, and so his institutions are *instrumentally* valuable. If it should come about that they cease to meet their instrumental aim, they can be varied or overridden. This flexibility provides the key. Locke draws his premises from a lived experience of politics, which reflects the plurality of conflicting values implicit in political life more accurately than the limited range of concerns available to neo-Kantian liberals. A liberalism of experience awake to the necessity of practical reason in political ethics and aware of the centrality for ethics of action over abstract consistency is better able to confront emergencies because it allows room for conflict and pluralism. It is no wonder that Locke's prerogative power of kings is the central account of emergency powers in the liberal canon.

But contemporary accounts of Locke's prerogative for the most part have failed to explain why this is so. I argue that the differing epistemological approaches of these different liberals are at the core of the capacity of some liberalisms and the incapacity of others to confront the problem of emergency.

What is at stake here is not simply a difference in epistemological approach, or the important difference in outcomes for emergency powers that each epistemological approach allows, critical as such outcomes might be. What is at stake is a core difference between moral outlooks, between what Stuart Hampshire has called "the acclaimed virtues of innocence and the undeniable virtues of experience."[14] To what degree is experience a valid mode of ethical life and ethical thought? Most philosophical liberalism is conducted in an innocent vein. Is there a way of doing political ethics that is alive to political experience?

Informed by the lessons of the previous chapters, Chapters 4 and 5 explore in more detail what a liberal ethics of emergency might look like. Such an ethics would follow Locke in treating institutions as originally, though not exclusively, of instrumental value and would be alive to political experience. It would confront the challenge of exceptionalism without succumbing to the conceptual framework of norms and exceptions. An ethics of emergency must also confront both illiberal elements of emergency powers: rights derogations, and mitigations of the rule of law. Chapter 4 targets the first of these, arguing for an ethical-political pluralism as an alternative to the political absolutism of exceptionalism and the normative absolutism of neo-Kantian liberalism.

I argue that justice and order (rights and liberal states) are inextricably bound, and that a metaphor of weighing and balancing is therefore inappropriate. Rights make little sense without states. Liberal ethics are actualized in order. Order is a countervailing principle, but not exactly a competing one.

It follows from this that the scope of liberal values is not coextensive with political ethics in general. Other values always play a role in the conduct of the state, no less under normal than under emergency circumstances. We tolerate day-to-day rights violations connected with criminal justice without question. I argue that these same values underlie emergency action, stressing that we should be no less smug or self-satisfied about rights violations in the first case than in the second.

---

[14] Hampshire, *Innocence and Experience*, p. 12.

Because it is not necessarily consistent, pluralism means moral tragedy, and while there may be a right thing to do, it may not be, in more abstract terms, right. Consistency need not come in theory. It is only *necessary* in the *practice* of ethics. Consistency can come through action. This allows that guilt and dirty hands are always a part of statesmanship and their weight should never be minimized, lest rights violations become too easy.

Liberal-democratic principles, because not comprehensive, should no more be rejected than classical mechanics, so long as theorists maintain a clear view of the doctrine's proper scope. Ethical pluralism of a practical kind provides a better model, not just for making and evaluating emergency decisions, but for ethical politics in general.

I will conclude from these discussions that the conception of an ethical raison d'état is appropriate only to a state with certain kinds of institutions, and that emergency powers are only just in certain kinds of states.

Chapter 5 addresses the other challenge of emergency powers: the mitigation of the rule of law. I use the institution of the Roman Dictatorship to illustrate continuity between normal and emergency powers with respect to power pluralism. Here as well a conceptual framework of norms and exceptions obscures the phenomena. The fate of the rule of law during states of emergency is a common concern among those who study emergency powers from a liberal or libertarian perspective. I argue that both in normal and emergency circumstances, power and its constraint are as much informal as formal, and hence we ought not to concentrate on the rule of law exclusively. In normal times, the rule of law is only one of a number of means of constraining and enabling. While the balance may shift, formal and informal power and constraint are continuous and not exceptional under emergency with respect to normal conditions.

Both those who praise the suspension of the rule of law in emergencies and those who reject it begin their account of crisis government with reference to the Roman Dictatorship. From Rousseau to Ackerman, theorists cite its speed, flexibility, and decisiveness to illustrate the shift from the rule of law to individual emergency rule. But this emergency institution is ill-understood and its use in the history of political thought serves to make a broader point about the study of crisis government. Normal rule of law versus *exceptional* individual rule constitutes a false and dangerous dichotomy. To make emergency institutions safer, we must not focus *solely* on the rule of law. Instead, effective emergency powers, which respect the values of uniformity and predictability that underlie the rule of law, can grow from a more complex understanding of constraint and enablement. As with Locke, we look to the moral end and to the empirically most moral but effective means. The chapter shows that Rome's Dictatorship better illustrates this complexity than the dichotomy in whose service it is normally invoked. While emergency powers enable rapid and effective action, we should focus on how this newly concentrated power can best be constrained from violating the underlying values of uniformity and predictability. The rule of law is instrumental to these more fundamental values, rather than intrinsically valuable. Because this is an extension of the way we think about power, risk, and enablement under normal circumstances, there is no radical difference in the structure of power between exceptional and normal circumstances. Emergencies require a shift subject to many of the same underlying principles that apply in normal circumstances, rather than a radical switch. We need make no exceptions.

States are only more or less under the rule of law. And, even under the most extreme constitutional emergency powers, states are never entirely subject to the sovereign will of an individual. Carl Schmitt's conception of sovereign dictatorship is impossible: as abstract and unworkable as liberal ideal theory. Institutions confer formal powers, but institutions and laws are among a number of means of constraining the informal flow of power. Any normative account of emergency powers that aims at safely optimizing liberal democratic values under emergency conditions will have to contend with this more complex landscape of risk and enablement. We focus on the rule of law alone at our peril.

Chapter 6 looks forward, gathering together the normative and institutional insights of the previous chapters to develop a set of principles for institutional design. I discuss two classes of institutions, those delineated in constitutions or laws and those Oren Gross has called "extra-legal measures," showing how neither approach is straightforwardly superior. Whether or not institutions for crisis government are optimally safe and effective depends primarily on the topography of power, how it flows and how this flow erodes and reshapes its banks.

I suggest that the necessity of further empirical investigation and propose some important variables to consider.

The pluralism I advocate in this book shows how we might navigate the Scylla of amoralist exceptionalism on one hand and the Charybdis of libertarian rejection of emergency powers on the other. Liberal and emergency principles and the values that drive them function together and function constantly. So, some uses of emergency powers under carefully specified conditions, and even when that use is tragic, might be justified after all. This book aims to help us think more clearly about how and when this might be the case.

New emergency provisions after September 11, 2001, prompted many citizens of liberal democracies the world over to question how to balance security and liberty.[15] As we shall see, the problem is both more complex and fundamental. All states need some provision for dealing effectively with emergency conditions. When faced with emergencies, states that are not equipped with formal powers use impromptu powers anyway, as the United States' history of martial law and executive decrees in wartime demonstrates. Arguably, those states with the most diffuse power structures under normal circumstances are most in need of emergency powers under extreme circumstances. Liberal democratic states are one kind of 'diffuse power' state, and hold accountability and individual rights as core values. This diffusion of power is simultaneously at the core of liberal democratic moral identity and the source of its vulnerability.

---

[15] Among the many books and articles that refer to the problem in this way are Amitai Etzioni, *Rights vs. Public Safety after September 11*; and Kent Roach. *September 11: Consequences for Canada*, p. 113. Ronald Dworkin has wisely pointed out that, given that the average American is unlikely to be subject to the provisions of such legislation as the USA PATRIOT Act, the balance in question is between some people's security and other people's liberty: see "Terror and the Attack on Civil Liberties," p. 1.

2

Must Exceptionalism Prove the Rule?

Let's begin by tracing the origins of exceptionalism in the history of political thought. There, as in contemporary theory, exceptionalism has been the dominant mode of confronting the problem of emergencies in constitutional regimes. As we shall see, the contemporary perception that states of exception are 'normally' time bound has lead to a critique that complains that states of exception have now come to prove the rule. I will show that this perspective is grounded in a failure to understand the fundamental nature of exceptionalism as a doctrine. Exceptionalism always implies a constantly exempted political figure, in contrast to democratic governance, which necessitates an always accountable political figure. By recognizing the implicit move toward permanent exemption, we see the merit in an alternative. While rights derogations may indeed be the rule, so is accountability when those rights derogations occur. Exceptionalism is a doctrine fundamentally incompatible with democratic accountability.

Hence the issue is not that states of exception now prove the rule, but rather that emergencies ought never to be conceptualized as exceptions to begin with. For, as I will argue in subsequent chapters, rights derogations are not temporally exceptional but rather are continuous with normal circumstances, and so if political leaders are to be held accountable in normal cases, why not in emergencies? Political leaders are never exempted from accountability when such derogations are made. Equating emergencies with exceptions, because emergencies necessitate such exemptions, is a dangerous game.

Exceptionalism is grounded in the claim that the usual norms cease to apply in emergencies. Exceptional times, as the saying goes, call for exceptional measures. Emergency powers, on a view that conflates them with exceptionalism, are amoral because a rule that does not apply cannot be violated. As we shall see, exceptionalism offers us a clear view of the challenge of emergencies, which liberal democratic government must face, although this view has little to offer in terms of solutions and much that liberals might fear. By suspending the norms against which their conduct might be measured, exceptionalist conceptions of emergency exempt government from accountability. But accountability is a central element of responsibility. Responsible government requires that political leaders act on behalf of their citizens and so answer to their citizens for their actions. If political leaders or their emergency actions are exempt from criteria of accountability, government ceases to be responsible, and liberal democracy ceases to be practicable. But those liberals who respond by claiming that our institutions are necessarily inflexible ignore rather than confront this challenge. Ultimately, we would do well to consider an alternative framework for understanding emergency.

I will illustrate two kinds of exceptionalism in the history of political thought, 'republican' and 'decisionist.' Since our aim is to understand the origins and logic of the modern exceptionalist perspective by means of examining instances of its careful articulation, it makes sense, on the one hand, to draw on those modern thinkers on the subject of emergency politics who have been the most influential. Machiavelli and Schmitt are the central figures here. But because Rousseau and Hobbes are such close relations of Machiavelli and Schmitt in their accounts of emergency, and because we own them within our own liberal and democratic traditions, it is a worthwhile exercise to show the ease with which the relevant concepts migrate.[1] Republican exceptionalism is informed by broader ideological aims, in particular the founding and preservation of a certain kind of state. It is exemplified in Machiavelli and Rousseau whose work exhibits a bifurcated ethics of emergency

---

[1] For this same reason, the chapter is organized thematically rather than chronologically. This is not an inquiry into the history of political thought in the strict sense of tracing the development of political ideas over time. Rather, I aim to explore a persistent cluster of ideas.

whose parts I term 'existential' and 'quotidian.' Existential ethics relate to founding or preserving a state while quotidian ethics govern life within a state. But it is apparent from the work of Rousseau and Machiavelli that the split between these kinds of ethics is not a temporal one because, in both men's work, emergency is constantly potential. It is not a question of *when* existential ethics apply but of *who* may apply them.[2]

Decisionist exceptionalism finds primary exemplars in Schmitt and Hobbes. With them, ideological aims are less central and instead, the imperatives of what I call decisionist logic come to the fore. 'Untrustworthy,' 'vicious,' and 'unpredictable' describe humans and their natural environment. Responding to a world that is not governed by norms by acting in accordance with rules and normative restrictions is a foolish endeavor. Moreover, deliberation, with the reliance on the judgment of groups of individuals that it suggests, would simply lead to further chaos. Only decisive and absolute sovereignty, entirely unrestricted by norms can effectively confront chaos. This kind of originary decision has distinctively religious as well as authoritarian overtones. Like the republican exceptionalists, decisionists connect special powers and exemption from everyday ethics with a specific office rather than with a temporally discrete condition. It should not be surprising, then, that decisionists are generally political absolutists.

Emergency is the permanent condition of humankind whether potentially or actually for exceptionalists of both types, and their politics and political ethics follow accordingly. Norm/exception is less a division of distinct temporal conditions – times of normalcy/times of emergency – than a status divide. Even a republican state requires a father figure or a statesman for whom the day-to-day ethics of the state is merely a means, a plebeian ethics. Norms are for normal people. What is distinctive about emergency, temporally speaking, is that it brings to the forefront – it brings into view – the constant undercurrent of this two-tier ethics. Exceptionalism allows emergency to puncture the

---

[2] Some scholars have suggested in recent years, without drawing the connection to Machiavelli's and Rousseau's republican exceptionalism, that this is exactly the case with regard to the national security powers of the President of the USA. See Jules Lobel, "Emergency Power and the Decline of Liberalism"; Kim Lane Scheppele, "Law in a Time of Emergency," p. 1015.

normal order by making explicit the more or less implicit moral divisions that are as central in the republican regimes of Rousseau and Machiavelli, as they are in the more authoritarian regime of Hobbes.

Hence, those thinkers who claim that states of exception were once time bounded, but are no longer so, are confused. While a state of emergency can refer to a discrete period of time, the notion of a time-bounded exceptionalism is incoherent. Exceptionalism is always exercised by some designated authority. No one suggests that there is ever a condition in which all are unconstrained by norms. Insofar as that authority that could be exempted from norms as such is always 'potentially exempted' and therefore never, strictly speaking, bound, it is the conceptualization of emergency as a state of exception in the first place that enables the dangers of exceptionalism.

The thinkers in this chapter take emergency deadly seriously whereas, with some notable exceptions, liberal thinkers have not. As a result, they have set the terms of debate. These terms exclude the possibility of accountability – a necessary and defining feature of responsible government – by suspending the norms against which state conduct might be measured. Because they exempt certain *exceptional* figures from ethics as we normally understand them, exceptionalism must be treated with caution as we set about exploring and evaluating its resources. Its rhetoric and its logic are dangerous in real world contexts.

To the extent that exceptionalism entails and is entailed by a set of assumptions antithetical to liberal values, we should be cautious in understanding emergency powers in this fashion. Awareness of the logical antecedents and consequents of exceptionalism, coupled with an awareness that it is not just a temptation of absolutists, but also of republicans and democrats, might help to offset some of its dangers. Confronting the conceptual structure of the exceptionalist rhetoric coloring so much contemporary discussion of emergency, on both the right and the left, is a first step toward the development of a more normatively and theoretically sound understanding of the apparent paradox of emergency.

EXISTENTIAL AND QUOTIDIAN ETHICS AND EXCEPTIONALISM

I want to begin by introducing a distinction that will play a significant role in the conceptual geography of my argument in this chapter. This is a distinction between existential and quotidian conditions and their corresponding ethics.

Existential and quotidian ethics are concerned with political order. We can think of a political order as an entity within which day-to-day ethical-political commitments and tasks are undertaken. Each order embodies, or perhaps is constituted by the quotidian ethics of its respective regime type. Across all the diversity of kinds of orders there is the constant that there be *some* normative criteria for social and political intercourse (and here I mean normative in the broadest possible sense, not strictly in the moral sense) and that there be a mechanism of enforcement. There is some set way in which things run, and there is widespread (though not full) compliance, backed up by the threat of consequences. Order refers both to the condition that obtains when the rules are honored or enforced and to the structure itself. We can speak of 'an order' and we can speak of maintaining or restoring order within 'an order.' Existential ethics are concerned with the existence of a functional regime. They concern conditions such as those at the moment of a state's creation, or moments at which its continuation is in question. Quotidian ethics constitute the substance of the structure and apply to the everyday tug of war of policy and politics. This is essentially a distinction between background or structuring political conditions, and foreground or quotidian political functions.

Quotidian political ethics function in accordance with the existing political order, while existential ethics invoke different and possibly higher order criteria to create or preserve that order. Quotidian ethics depend on the character of the order itself and vary significantly. An order necessarily has moral content when it is made actual in the world, and different values infuse and structure different orders. The quotidian ethics of a Maoist regime are significantly different from those of contemporary Sweden. This is not in the least to imply some kind of relativism. It is not to say that there is nothing to choose between these different regime types. I mean only that what counts as just *within* a regime depends substantially on the character of that regime as exemplified through its stated values and the values that infuse its structure. This does not preclude argument about the second-order worthiness of its stated values and its moral character in general. Quotidian ethics concern the stated values of a regime in its actuality, and its character is constituted by these ethics.

Order is simultaneously the structure and that which steadies the structure, and existential ethics are those ethics concerned with building or steadying the structure. Existential ethics, as opposed to quotidian ethics, are characterized by their relative uniformity across regime types. They are goal directed in that they are concerned with the preservation of the structure in which order is normally maintained. Under various systems of emergency legislation, it is common to find some reference to the inability of existing ordering forces – for instance, the police – to manage the crisis. The fact that normal means of managing an emergency are unavailable is almost tautological: when the order through which norms and laws are normally enforced is threatened, the order itself is threatened. If the very existence of the state or the way of life enjoyed within it is at risk, it is often simultaneously, because of this threat, unable to help itself through normal means. It is this central moment that we might call politically existential, and the ethics that correspond to such a condition are existential ethics.[3]

In what follows, we shall see that decisionist and republican exceptionalists have, as a central difference, the status of existential ethics. Republican exceptionalists recognize and rely upon existential ethics, and this kind of exceptionalism is therefore an exceptionalism specifically from quotidian ethics. Decisionist exceptionalism, on the other hand, is of a more fundamental kind insofar as existential conditions are not governed by existential ethics. For decisionists, exception is from ethics as such. As a corollary, we shall see that decisionist exceptionalists are less concerned about the moral content of the order in the first place, and hence would lack any *moral* justification for emergency action.

REPUBLICAN EXCEPTIONALISM

By 'republican exceptionalism' I mean to denote a kind of exceptionalism that provides an implicit justification for what I have called

---

[3] It is important to note that not all emergencies are existential. Even if the citizens of a whole region of a state are seriously threatened, this would not necessarily mean that the state itself was under threat. A good rule of thumb might be the criterion that a threat, because of its urgency and scale, goes beyond the capacity of the normal ordering forces, for example beyond the capacity of police with normal powers, to manage.

existential ethics. This justification comes in the form of an appeal to the moral excellence of a well-formed republic. A well-formed republic is, on this view, a particularly desirable kind of order because of the particularly desirable kind of quotidian ethics it enables. Existential ethics, here, are justified because the republican state is a condition of the good life or the moral life in general, whether individually or collectively. It is not surprising, then, that the two key protagonists of such a view are those great republicans Rousseau and Machiavelli.[4] I want to establish three claims with relation to these thinkers. First, I want to show that they implicitly subscribe to the division between quotidian and existential ethics that I have been describing. Second, I will illustrate how this entails an exceptionalism that is distinctly republican. Finally, I want to suggest that the existential/quotidian distinction each employs does not correspond to a temporal divide.

In the political theory of Machiavelli and Rousseau, the distinction between quotidian and existential ethics and its relationship to emergency is everywhere evident, but rarely explicit. It is perhaps for this reason that it has received comparatively little attention.[5] Both rely on the distinction as a core premise of their respective systems, as the accounts here should make clear.

Machiavelli and Rousseau employ a clearly delineated separation between the ethics governing the establishment and maintenance of states and the radically different ethics that regulate daily life within a state. The founders and protectors of good regimes are accorded

---

[4] The question of whether Machiavelli is a republican in the first place, and what kind of republican he might be is not a settled one. The copious literature on Machiavelli's republicanism includes: Mary Dietz, "Trapping the Prince: Machiavelli and the Politics of Deception"; Mark Hulliung, *Citizen Machiavelli*; J. G. A. Pocock, *The Machiavellian Moment: Florentine Political Thought and the Atlantic Republican Tradition*; Sheldon Wolin, *Politics and Vision*. Alternatively, see Leo Strauss in his *Thoughts on Machiavelli*.

[5] Most major interpreters of Machiavelli give some consideration to the figure of the Founder in his work. Hannah Pitkin, for instance, devotes a chapter to the subject in *Fortune Is a Woman*, and Wolin discusses this aspect of Machiavelli in *Politics and Vision*, p. 231. Pocock deals briefly with the "ideal type of the legislator" in *The Machiavellian Moment*, pp. 171–2. Isaiah Berlin comes closest to addressing the special moral status of this figure in his "The Originality of Machiavelli," where he refers to two implicit, complete, separate systems of ethics, "not two autonomous regions, one of ethics, another of politics" (p. 58). Judith Shklar's *Men and Citizens* also hints at this line of interpretation of Rousseau. For an account of the relationship of Machiavelli to contemporary executive prerogative see Harvey Mansfield, *Taming the Prince*.

different prerogatives from those accorded to citizens. Machiavelli's and Rousseau's theatres of state are populated by characters who act out this distinction.[6] These include Rousseau's Legislator and Wolmar in his novel *La nouvelle Héloise*, as well as Émile's tutor, Machiavelli's founders and invigorators of states, and the dictator advocated by both. These characters share the important feature of a prerogative to engage in morally circumscribed activities for the purpose of establishing or preserving a sphere of (some kind of) quotidian political ethics.

MACHIAVELLI'S FOUNDERS

For Machiavelli, the existential/quotidian distinction and his ideas about extraordinary figures and their prerogatives in founding or maintaining a state are bound up with his conception of time and of history. The normal course of political life and the normal ethics within it will fall into degradation. The same institutions that are excellent when the people are virtuous are detrimental when the people become corrupt.[7] The temporal tends toward the corruption of the body politic, though time, for Machiavelli, is cyclic over all.[8] It is not simply entropic, though it is destructive for any particular entity; there is a life *cycle*, but for any given entity there is only death. So, with states, if they last long enough, which Machiavelli thinks unlikely anyway, "they will be apt to revolve indefinitely in the circle of revolutions" between different forms of government.[9] Machiavelli's philosophy of history and time could be aptly described as a secularization of theological or messianic time, in that his aim is to disrupt or puncture this cycle: a republic has to be reestablished or "brought back to its original principles from time to time" and

---

[6] It would be interesting to catalogue and contrast the metaphors of political theorists and explore their preconditions and ramifications. The ship of state with its helmsman and captain is familiar from Plato up to the present day. We are also, of course, very familiar with the metaphor of the body politic from Aristotle to Hobbes and onward. But, for Rousseau and Machiavelli, the state might best be described as a theatre populated by characters and brought alive through performance. We are perhaps more used to the theater metaphor with reference to battle, a matter worth pondering.

[7] Niccolò Machiavelli, *Discourses*, in *The Prince and Discourses*, bk I, ch. 18. Rousseau and Machiavelli citations refer to book and chapter number.

[8] Machiavelli, *Discourses*, I.49, I.59, III.8.

[9] Machiavelli, *Discourses*, I.2.

so founding is an ongoing activity.[10] Even the best institutions fall into corruption, as Rousseau also expects. The aim, however, is to maintain the good forms of government and the quotidian virtue they make possible, and hence the state as a whole, for as long as possible.

To stall this process is difficult. One could alter the institutions to suit the changing condition of the people. The institutions appropriate to a noble people are no longer appropriate once the people are corrupted. Unfortunately, this requires both an exceptional citizen to notice the corrosion of political life in time *and* that his fellow citizens are able to recognize his authority in this matter. Machiavelli considers this next to impossible.[11]

In the third book of the *Discourses* he suggests another means of offsetting or at least slowing the otherwise certain decay. This is his famous idea of bringing a state back to its founding through a shocking display.[12] A renewer of republican virtue must do as Machiavelli's founders do: Moses, Solon, Lycurgus, and Brutus exercise sheer human agency to rupture the normal part-entropic, part-cyclic flow of time. To bring about the sought-after effect, the situation requires, for Machiavelli, a display of violence. (We might say: the cathartic role of the theatrical is here revived.) Human action must rip through the normal course of events. It must be a visceral experience. Machiavelli describes a number of cases of shocking violence that achieve a kind of renewal or cleansing. For example, there is the case of the Florentine magistrates of the mid-fifteenth century, who would "resume the government" every five years, by renewing the sense of fear and awe in the people through some horrible public punishment.[13] Something shocking reawakens citizens to first principles and thus preserves them. This something shocking, however, sits badly with quotidian ethics.

A central case is that of Brutus, who kills his own sons in founding the republic.[14] In the name of ordering the Romagna, an existential political task, Machiavelli will forgive Cesare Borgia for chopping his henchman in half.[15] Romulus is forgiven the murder of his brother because of the

[10] Machiavelli, *Discourses*, III.1.
[11] Machiavelli, *Discourses*, I.17, I.18.
[12] Machiavelli, *Discourses*, III.1.
[13] Machiavelli, *Discourses*, III.1.
[14] Machiavelli, *Discourses*, III.3.
[15] Machiavelli, *The Prince*, p. vii.

existential nature of his aims.[16] Agathocles, on the other hand, is chastised, because his goal is purely self-serving.[17] Absent a republican aim, only quotidian ethics should govern his actions, without prerogative.

Machiavelli's founders are also liars. In his discussion of the usefulness of religion in the *Discourses*, he emphasizes that a ruler should do everything to increase the religiosity of his people so that they might be "consequently well conducted and united."[18] This is so even if the religion is a false one. Miracles, if they can be arranged, are particularly useful. "For the sagacious rulers have given these miracles increased importance, no matter whence or how they originated; and their authority afterwards gave them credence with the people."[19]

Machiavelli will only conscience violence and lies for a *worthy* political end. If one's aim is to found or restore the state, then one has a wide prerogative. His founders and law-givers and his renewers of republican virtue are in a sense 'out of order' and there is a sense in which they are also 'out of time.' Existential ethics are always available to such figures. They are never constrained by the quotidian.

That there are two ethics at work here is further underlined when Machiavelli specifically raises the question of whether Romulus set a bad example in having killed his brother, among other crimes. Machiavelli's interlocutor

will urge that, if such actions be justifiable, ambitious citizens who are eager to govern, may follow the example of their prince and use violence against those who are opposed to their authority. A view that will hold good provided we leave out of consideration the end which Romulus had in committing these murders.[20]

It is not for just any reason that these actions are condoned, but exactly because they serve the creation or renewal of the state. Good ends involve the common good in the form of republican virtue, not the satisfaction of a man's own ambition. It is for this reason that other murderous figures, such as Giovanpaolo, are culpable while the

---

[16] Machiavelli, *Discourses*, I.9.
[17] Machiavelli, *The Prince*, p. viii.
[18] Machiavelli, *Discourses*, I.12.
[19] Machiavelli, *Discourses*, I.12.
[20] Machiavelli, *Discourses*, I.9.

founders are not.[21] Note that this is not a utilitarian morality. It is not the case that the good of the founding simply outweighs the evil of the murder. Machiavelli is dealing with absolute goods and absolute evils that are not quantifiable or measurable.

In Machiavelli's work, exceptional figures are exempted from the normal moral-legal-religious order. At the same time, order continues to govern everyday popular life. The state, on this view, is constantly in danger, and "princes and magistrates . . . must watch all points."[22] The state must be continually maintained by one who is beyond the reach of everyday norms. The exceptional figure, but only the exceptional figure, acts according to existential ethics because his aim is the moral aim of establishing or preserving the worthy state. Machiavelli favors *liberta* over *tirranica*. Principalities are not incompatible with good government, but the most glorious, the most virtuous, the most lasting, the most conducive to public welfare, and the most free form of government is a well-constructed republic.[23] What makes the republic a moral end from Machiavelli's perspective is its capacity to further these values. Hence, his is a republican exceptionalism.

ROUSSEAU'S FOUNDERS

In his discussion of the Legislator in Book II of the *Social Contract*, Rousseau draws heavily on Machiavelli's ideas about the existential prerogative of founders and shares the implicit acceptance of the distinction between existential and quotidian political ethics. Recognizing this provides a means of making sense of some peculiar contradictions in Rousseau's work. Rousseau tells us that one of the aims of the social compact is to substitute "a moral and legitimate equality for that physical inequality with which nature can distinguish men."[24] The passionate faith that Rousseau exhibits in such an equality is everywhere evident in his writings. Nonetheless there are characters whom Rousseau paints as superior beings: a Legislator in the *Social Contract*, the tutor of Émile, and Wolmar in *La nouvelle Héloise* are all figures whose

---

[21] Machiavelli, *Discourses*, I.27.
[22] Machiavelli, *Discourses*, I.33.
[23] Machiavelli, *Discourses*, III.7.
[24] Jean-Jacques Rousseau, *Du contrat social*, I.9. Unless otherwise noted, Rousseau translations are my own.

superiority and even godlike quality Rousseau clearly intends to convey. There is equality among men in general, but not between them and the great founders and preservers of states.

The Legislator is one of the more interesting characters in Rousseau's menagerie. He is:

> in every respect an extraordinary man in the state. If he must be such by reason of his genius, he is no less so by reason of his endeavor. It is not exactly magistracy, nor exactly sovereignty. This endeavor, which constitutes the republic, does not exactly enter into its constitution. It is a particular and superior function that has nothing in common with the human domain.[25]

Rousseau draws his notion of the Legislator from the legendary legislators of antiquity. As a child, his father had read to him from Plutarch. Rousseau's love of Sparta grew partly from a love of Lycurgus, and, indeed, Lycurgus serves as the chief example in the chapter on the Legislator in the *Social Contract*. The job of the Legislator is to give the republic a constitution. Because the constitution effectively creates the state, the Legislator effectively creates the state. The state is a set of institutions, but these institutions are not simply rules and offices. Rather, institutions determine character. "Anyone who presumes to give institutional form to a people [*d'instituer un peuple*] must feel himself to be in a condition to change, so to speak, human nature."[26]

Rousseau does not mince words in describing the sheer superiority of the Legislator over other types of humans. In fact, he calls him godlike.[27] Only someone who knows and loves humanity but is not afflicted by its ills can make laws for it. The Legislator is outside the normal order, is given powers of creation, and is charged with the preservation and happiness of his people.

---

[25] Rouseau, *Du contrat social*, II.7.

[26] Rouseau, *Du contrat social*, II.7.

[27] Rouseau, *Du contrat social*, II.7. Either Rousseau is speaking rhetorically, or else he means to suggest that people can never have good laws. He refers to many human legislators and to restraints placed upon them. Moreover, Rousseau himself acts the part of the Legislator when he writes a constitution for Poland, and indeed in writing *Du contrat social* itself. His description of the Legislator as godlike perhaps serves the rhetorical function of underlining his extraordinary moral status. See Rousseau, *The Government of Poland*.

This Legislator is extraordinary in another, related sense. He is permitted to engage in sketchy activities by virtue of his capacity as founder. Rousseau holds – explicitly following Machiavelli – that the Legislator must have recourse to appeals to divine will if his constitution is to be embraced by the citizen-sovereigns.[28] This is, effectually, a claim to an entitlement to dupe and manipulate the people. It is a claim to a noble lie.[29] That such a thing could be allowed by Rousseau is particularly interesting given his driving hatred for deception and inauthenticity.[30]

In Rousseau's menagerie the Legislator is echoed in several other figures, particularly Émile's tutor and Wolmar, the man who marries Julie in Rousseau's sentimental novel *La nouvelle Héloise*. Wolmar rules his model estate benevolently, and in a fashion designed to lessen everyone's awareness of rank and condition, but he himself is godlike: he refashions men's souls and brings peace, stability, and happiness.[31] He could embody no more clearly the strange tension between the love of equality and Rousseau's apparent passion for the exceptional, superior man.

Jean-Jacques, the tutor in *Émile* could also be cast as a superior man: a perfect Legislator for Émile, whom we can understand as the city writ small for the self-absorbed philosopher. Jean-Jacques is constantly manipulating his little charge:

Let him always believe that he is the master, and let it always be you who are. There is no subjection so perfect as that which keeps the appearance of freedom ... He ought to do only what he wants; but he ought to only want what you want him to do. He ought not to make a step without your having foreseen it; he ought not to open his mouth without your knowing what he is going to say.[32]

---

[28] Rousseau, *Du contrat social*, I.7.

[29] Such a claim has a very illustrious history, of course.

[30] "How sweet it would be to live among us, if our faces showed our heart's true disposition!" Rousseau's *Discours sur les sciences et les arts* (Paris: Garnier-Flammarion, 1971, p. 32) gives his clearest statement of this love of authenticity, but it is equally apparent in his multiple autobiographies.

[31] Shklar, *Men and Citizens*, p. 136.

[32] Jean-Jacques Rousseau, *Émile*, p. 120. Arguably, all liberal democratic governments see their interest in restricting and promoting certain sorts of behavior without commanding. Attempts to provide incentives and disincentives take the form of, for instance, tax benefits or penalties, but they also make their way into public education, public health services, etc. Since Foucault we have come to recognize that yet more sinister forces are work. See, for instance, *Discipline and Punish*.

Hence the tutor also functions as a figure in the realm of existential ethics. He behaves in a manner almost despicable in an effort to create conditions for Émile to function as an autonomous moral creature. In each case, the purpose of the ethical prerogatives enjoyed by Rousseau's figures is to establish a republican ethical political order and to enable good and meaningful moral lives, within which different political ethics will govern the interactions of citizens with each other and with their government (or, of Émile with himself and with the world). The Legislator is exempt from the normal moral order for the good of its existence.

DICTATORSHIP

Both Machiavelli and Rousseau are enthusiastic, if wary supporters of another political figure with prerogative. Although the dictator fills an office that is part of Machiavelli's *ordini* and an explicit element of Rousseau's constitution, he nonetheless works within the sphere of existential political ethics. He fulfils the role of surrogate Tutor/Legislator/Founder. Their dictator, modeled on the Roman emergency magistracy, which will be discussed at length in Chapter 5, differs from the others in that his role is clearly defined. There is no deception or manipulation involved. The dictator is constitutionally sanctioned. The exceptional figure can grow out of the normal order, not just institute it.

Rousseau states unequivocally: "the prime concern of the people is that the state shall not perish."[33] Once the state exists, it is imperative to act to maintain it. "A thousand cases unforeseen by the Legislator could present themselves."[34] Émile tells his tutor on his passage to fatherhood, "As long as I live, I shall need you."[35] The distinction between existential and quotidian or normal is thus not a temporal one. While the little state that is Émile comes eventually to function on his own, he needs his guardian lurking in the background for guidance and advice, in case, for instance, of emergency.

It is still a commonplace that dictators decide while democracies dither. Rousseau admires the dictator for these reasons, which closely

---

[33] Rousseau, *Du contrat social*, IV.6.
[34] Rousseau, *Du contrat social*, IV.6.
[35] Rousseau, *Émile*, p. 480.

resemble those of the Roman republican constitutional thinkers and of Machiavelli. For all three, the ever present and, over time, almost inevitable, possibility of an emergency meant that the republic required flexibility, which here means the intrusion of existential ethics into the day-to-day functioning of the state, if it is not to be destroyed. Machiavelli neatly puts it thus: "republics which, when in imminent danger, have recourse neither to a dictatorship, nor to some form of authority analogous to it, will always be ruined when grave misfortune befalls them."[36] There must be a crack in the rule of law wide enough for an extraordinary figure to step through when the circumstances call for it. Otherwise, the state is in serious danger. Still, for Rousseau, "only the gravest emergencies . . . can balance out the dangers of altering the public order and the sacred power of the laws," which should only be circumvented when *"il s'agit au salut de la patrie."*[37]

Notwithstanding both Rousseau's and Machiavelli's fascination with Roman political institutions in general, the dictatorship is a peculiar institution for them to embrace, however cautiously. The dictator, at least as they understand him, is an exceptional figure, not governed by the usual normative restrictions or even the rule of everyday law. His activities are bounded only by the restriction that he must not change the constitution and by the task he has been set.[38] The constitution itself allows for its own suspension, for the suspension of quotidian norms in exceptional cases.

For both Rousseau and Machiavelli, the existential ethics according to which the statesman or legislator acts to found and preserve have the glory of a republic and its values as their fundamental justification. They recognize a bifurcated ethics, one that exempts the Legislator or statesman from the normal rules of ethical conduct so that he may go about founding or preserving a republican state that is ever presently in danger. Because the state enables everything good, in other words because, for Machiavelli, and in a different sense for Rousseau also, there is nothing good without the state, the Legislator may do *anything* to create or maintain it. For both thinkers, although in different ways,

---

[36] Machiavelli, *Discourses*, I.34.
[37] Rousseau, *Du contrat social*, IV.6.
[38] But in fact this is a misconception. The dictator's duties are not bound in these ways after all. See Chapter 5.

the state is central to the existence and functioning of worthwhile daily life.[39] This justifies existential ethics, which govern emergency conduct even when normal ethics do not apply. Norms still govern the abnormal situation, but not the same norms.

For Machiavelli, a state's mode of founding is critical to its character and the political conditions within it. In the *Discourses*, Machiavelli tells us that it is because of its laws that Rome lasted so long.[40] The character of the institutions set up by the legislators, Romulus and Numa, determined the character of the inhabitants. In founding the state, which, for Machiavelli, means creating its institutions, the political character of its inhabitants is also influenced.[41]

If the state is such a transformative ethical force, ethics within the state cannot be the same as ethics outside the state. If the state alters relationships and creates entitlements and duties, then what is required of one and what is owed are obviously different within and without. Indeed, for Rousseau at least, what one *is* is different within and without. Republican virtue is not possible outside of the state, nor, for Rousseau, is justice. Hence, for many republican thinkers, the coming into existence of the state *itself* serves as a moral imperative governing action under existential political circumstances. Kant, for example, held the social contract to be a categorical imperative, because of what is made possible, ethically speaking, within the state.[42] Machiavelli sees the moral obligation to found a state differently than does Kant, insofar

---

[39] Rousseau, *Du contrat social*, I.8, and I.9; Machiavelli, *Discourses*, III.29.

[40] Machiavelli, *Discourses*, I.1.

[41] The effect of institutions on human character in Machiavelli would be worthy of careful study. Given that Machiavelli holds that a people can become corrupted, it cannot be the case that he thinks republican government changes human nature. On this point, the dispute between Pocock and Vicki Sullivan is interesting. Pocock suggests in *The Machiavellian Moment* that a core aspect of the republicanism of Machiavelli's day is that the "experience of citizenship ... had changed their natures in a way that mere custom had not ... it was the end of man to be a citizen or political animal, it was his original nature or *prima forma* that was developed, and developed irreversibly, by the experience of the *vivere civile*" (p. 184). Sullivan is convincing to the extent that it is a stretch to suggest Machiavelli's republicanism is grounded in the benefits for self-actualization that political participation provides. See Vicki Sullivan, "Machiavelli's Momentary 'Machiavellian Moment': A Reconsideration of Pocock's Treatment of the Discourses." Nonetheless, Machiavelli clearly and explicitly favors the *vita liberta* over *tirranica*, and he clearly associates the former with a republican form of government.

[42] Immanuel Kant, *The Metaphysics of Morals*, s. 44, p. 123.

as he has little interest in duties of a Kantian kind. Nor does Machiavelli, like Rousseau, see the state as explicitly changing human nature (as opposed to character). But the republican state is the route to greatness and glory. "Those who read what the beginning of Rome was, and what her law givers and her organization, will not be astonished that so much virtue should have maintained itself during so many centuries."[43] For Rousseau, the republican state is a utopian ideal, but it is *ideal* primarily because of its moral value.

Thus, the emergency exceptionalism of Rousseau and Machiavelli is a republican exceptionalism.[44] Soul and city are not so distinct. Rousseau and Machiavelli exemplify a position in which the existence of the state is necessary to certain kinds of ethics, where these ethics have the character of republican ethics, and where 'normal' or 'quotidian' ethics, embodied by and upheld within the state, are dependent upon a secondary mode of ethics, which I have called 'existential.'

But because the state is constantly in danger, the split between these different ethics, between (quotidian) norm and (existential) exception is not temporal but individual. There must *always* be someone who is not bound by quotidian norms because crisis could arise at any moment. In Rousseau, these exceptional figures generally have the character of wise and contemplative men and things move slowly in Rousseau's political universe. We have the impression of a parent watching a playing child from a window. Lackadaisical as it may be, supervision is constant. In Machiavelli, for whom politics in all of its gory minutiae was more of a delight and a calling, parenting is no idyll. The exceptional intrudes permanently on the normal in a more immediate and explosive way. In Isaiah Berlin's famous essay on "The Originality of Machiavelli," he agrees with Sheldon Wolin

that Machiavelli believes in a permanent 'economy of violence' – the need for a consistent reserve of force always in the background to keep things going in

---

[43] Machiavelli, *Discourses*, I.1.

[44] From this perspective, we can see that those American scholars like Kim Lane Scheppele who have called the Bush administration's response to 9/11 'Schmittian' have got it half right. Exceptionalism need not be of the Schmittian variety, and insofar as the aim is specifically to "save the republic" as opposed to "to obliterate the existential threat," the Bush administration's approach may best be described as republican exceptionalism. See Scheppele, "Law in a Time of Emergency."

such a way that the virtues admired by him and by the classical thinkers to whom he appeals can be protected and allowed to flower.[45]

It is the permanence of the economy of violence, the "as long as I live I shall need you,"[46] that makes the difference. Rousseau and Machiavelli both confront the problem of emergency through this constant functioning of a statesman's existential and popular quotidian ethics.

DECISIONISM

Autoritas Non Veritas

Of the two branches of exceptionalism that define a major part of the history of political thought on the subject of emergencies, decisionism is the more troubling and puzzling.[47] While republican exceptionalists approach emergency as a moral matter, with exception from quotidian ethics only, the logic of decisionism avoids any ideological stance, entailing a more comprehensive exceptionalism. For, in the absence of a Great Good that the state serves, existential ethics have no content.

Decisionism describes the view that, in politics, sovereign power is defined by having the final say. This final say is not dictated by law or rule, nor is it subject to law or rule. It is wholly original to the power in question. Hence, an executive who *applies* the law that a legislature makes is not a decisionist figure. The decisionist ruler must be the *source* of law, as diktat. His must be "the Decision [*Dezision*] in absolute purity."[48]

Decisionism serves as the conclusion of a logical progression. It begins with a conception of human nature and of human circumstances as chaotic and violent. Some, but not all, decisionists conceive of this chaos as only apparent, as the manifestation of God's logic, which we

---

[45] Berlin, "The Originality of Machiavelli," pp. 66.
[46] Rousseau, *Émile*, p. 480.
[47] It is interesting to note that there are a number of apolitical or only marginally political decisionists. In addition to some of those already mentioned, we might add Paul Tillich, Pascal, and Kierkegaard. Their decisionism is still theological.
[48] Carl Schmitt, *Political Theology*, p. 19.

are unable or not intended to discern,[49] or of a world too complicated for geometrical and scientific method yet to master. Hence, decisionists define themselves in opposition to the normal in general, since norms are indeterminable. Chaos and violence are unpredictable and this renders effective government impossible under normative strictures, which would severely limit the means of maintaining order. Norms are appropriate to the normal situation only, and the normal situation, to the extent that it exists, is always temporary and barely contained. For decisionists, it follows from this permanent potential emergency that there must always be a central, unitary, and incontrovertible power, the source of all law and its guarantor, and hence, one above the law. This figure is an absolute sovereign.

While the republican exceptionalists emphasized the value of what was to be preserved, and while that value stemmed from the embodiment of principles of republican government, the decisionist shares no such patriotic or republican sentiment. The decisionist's aims are either more mundane – basic security and the enforcement of order – or more divine – as with those decisionists who see sovereign power as the divine essence realized on earth.

The relationship of decisionism to existential and quotidian ethics is more complex because the decisionist takes the prohibition of norms in the exceptional condition to be of greater profundity and seriousness than does the republican exceptionalist. This is not an exception from normal ethics only, but from ethics in general. Decisionists, therefore, cannot be said to invoke an existentialist ethics, at least not straightforwardly.

Decisionism is famously associated with Carl Schmitt, the great Weimar jurist and political thinker, and it is his ideas that primarily color contemporary theorists' claims about 'the exception.' As Schmitt tells us, his doctrine has long roots, extending back to Hobbes, through Donoso Cortes, and Maistre. I begin with an account of Schmitt's decisionist exceptionalism. I will then turn to Hobbes who presents an intriguing contrast. I employ Schmitt's critique of Hobbes to show the biconditionality of decisionists' assumptions and conclusions. To the extent that we do not wish to accept its assumptions, we ought to steer clear of its exceptionalist conclusions.

---

[49] As we find in the work of Joseph de Maistre, for example.

SCHMITT

"Souverän ist, wer über den Ausnahmezustand entscheidet"

A brief account of Schmitt's critique of liberal democracy effectively illustrates decisionist logic.[50] Much of Schmitt's important work was written in the short, sorry course of the Weimar Republic, when the fragile young liberal state teetered between the blows of the communists on the left and of Hitler's National Socialists on the right.[51] Schmitt, as a 'young conservative,' reserved a special loathing for the communists, although before 1933, he was no friend of Hitler's either. His hatred of liberal democracy, in practical terms, stemmed from its inability to confront these fundamental enemies.

Liberal democracy, on Schmitt's view, fails on at least three counts. Its openness paves the way to destructive forces within the state. Its diffuse power structure makes it impossible to effectively address such forces, and its insistence on the constant and ubiquitous functioning of liberal norms, even under exceptional conditions, fails to recognize that these are impossible without a guarantor of order.

Liberal openness exacerbates the potential for chaos that liberal separation of powers makes difficult to manage. Even the communist party and the Nazi Party were permitted to participate actively in Weimar parliamentary politics. That a state could be neutral toward a group whose explicit intention was to use this neutrality and this electoral system to acquire power for the sole purpose of destroying that system was proof of the state's fundamental incapacity, on Schmitt's view. The liberal-democratic neutral regime is helpless under such conditions of total enmity, a fundamental threat to the state's existence. Given Schmitt's definition of the political as grounded in

---

[50] Schmitt, *Political Theology*, p. 13. A startlingly similar sentiment was expressed in the British parliament, with respect to Charles I's Ship Money scandal in the 1640s: "If the Kinge be the judge of the necessitye, we have nothing and are but Tennants at will." Quoted in Tom Sorrel (ed.), *The Cambridge Companion to Hobbes*, p. 27.

[51] A useful overview of the culture and politics of Germany this time is provided in Anton Kaes, Martin Jay, and Edward Dimendberg (eds.), *The Weimar Republic Sourcebook*. An excellent account and critique of the struggles among Weimar legal theorists and the political ramifications of these struggles is David Dyzenhaus's *Legality and Legitimacy: Carl Schmitt, Hans Kelsen, and Hermann Heller in Weimar*. See also Peter Caldwell, *The Theory and Practice of Weimar Constitutionalism*.

the friend/enemy distinction, the liberal democratic regime's incapacity in the face of enmity, in the face of exception, is fundamentally a political incapacity.

It is exactly such conditions of enmity that Schmitt defines as 'exceptional.'[52] A state of exception is characterized by its unpredictability and its totality.[53] In contrast with a simple emergency, it is a condition of "extreme peril, a danger to the existence of the state."[54] While an emergency is any old condition of urgency – what we might call a quotidian problem – a state of exception concerns an existential condition. To understand the centrality of this difference, it might be helpful to consider it in grammatical terms. What is at issue in a state of exception is the subject, rather than some predicate of the subject. That which is might come not to be. Annihilation is not a more extreme form of damage, but fundamentally of a different category since it affects the subject, and not the predicates. For Schmitt, those threats that concern existence warrant 'states of exception' whereas those threats that concern predicates, we might say, constitute emergencies, which Schmitt terms '*Not*' in opposition to '*Ausnahmezustand*.'

Because the exception concerns the subject, and not its predicates, it has no determinate metaphysical reality. It can have an infinite number of concrete manifestations. The exception has no characteristics. One cannot tell in advance what circumstances might arise. Hence, what Ferejohn and Pasquino have aptly called the ontological view of emergencies – that exceptions are determinate and that, therefore, there can be laws or norms governing a decision on a state of exception – is impossible.[55] On this view, being mistaken about an emergency or an exception would be similar to being mistaken about whether a fruit was an orange or a lime: plausible, but we would seek some explanation in a defect of perception rather than in the subtle character of the object itself. Schmitt, instead, embraces what Ferejohn and Pasquino term the epistemological view. It is not a matter of simple application of a rule. It is not dictated by norms or governed by norms. It is constituted through a decision, and not according to criteria. Even the decision to suspend

---

[52] Carl Schmitt, *The Crisis of Parliamentary Democracy*, p. 36.
[53] Schmitt, *Political Theology*, p. 13.
[54] Schmitt, *Political Theology*, pp. 6, 12.
[55] John Ferejohn and Pasquale Pasquino, "The Law of Exception: A Typology of Emergency Powers," p. 226.

political ethics, for Schmitt, "emanates from nothingness."[56] It is wholly original.

It is specifically in this case that decision and sovereignty become relevant, exactly *because* norms, on Schmitt's view, bear a strained relationship to such conditions. The liberal democratic bias toward the centrality of law and normative principles is incapable of confronting extreme circumstances. Schmitt holds that "All law is 'situational law.'"[57] Norms apply only to the normal situation. When the sovereign has decided that a situation is exceptional, ethics are suspended. That ethics have no part to play in the decision itself shows the permanent potential of emergency. Just as existential ethics functions constantly, according to republican exceptionalists, so, for Schmitt (at least after 1923), a norm-less situation is the screen onto which daily life is projected.

Here arises the next problem with liberal democracy, on Schmitt's view. The liberal obsession with norms and with the rule of law, with distinct and separate spheres of jurisdictional authority, is exactly contrary to that which is necessary for confronting enmity and the exceptional case. There is too much discussion and the suffocating constriction of rules and of checks and balances. Schmitt tells us that "The precondition as well as the content of jurisdictional competence in such a case [i.e., a state of exception] must necessarily be unlimited. From a liberal constitutional point of view, there would be no jurisdictional competence at all."[58] For Schmitt, the liberal democratic regime is indecisive and weak. In his discussion of Donoso Cortés in *Political Theology* he quips that liberalism faced with 'Christ or Barabbas?' convenes a committee to discuss the problem.[59]

Exceptional government (which is constantly potential) must be characterized by "unlimited authority, which means the suspension of the entire existing order."[60] If laws can't govern, if regular police action is insufficient to maintain order, then there must be rule by decision, and not by norm. The person who decides whether such a situation exists is called sovereign, on Schmitt's view. The sovereign is the

---

[56] Schmitt, *Political Theology*, p. 32.
[57] Schmitt, *Political Theology*, p. 13.
[58] Schmitt, *Political Theology*, p. 7.
[59] Schmitt, *Political Theology*, p. 62.
[60] Schmitt, *Political Theology*, pp. 6, 12.

final guarantor of 'situational law.' The normative elements of liberal democracy are impossible on their own. "To create tranquility, security, and order, and thereby establish the normal situation, is the prerequisite for legal norms to be valid. Every norm presupposes the normal situation and no norm can be valid in an entirely abnormal situation."[61] Order is prerequisite for justice, on this view, with a clear lexical order. Therefore, the sovereign is not bound by moral restrictions. His central task is the preservation of the state, and, in the case of a commissarial dictator,[62] he is utterly goal directed, bound only by his own perception of that goal and how most efficiently to meet it. The *Zweckmäßigkeit* or end-appropriateness of the means is its only criterion.[63]

As in Machiavelli and Rousseau, these existential moments bleed into the quotidian in part because every quotidian moment is potentially existential and in part because the choice between *Not* and *Ausnahmezustand* is not necessarily straightforward. Whereas in his book *Die Diktatur* Schmitt argued for a commissarial dictator like that of the Romans, and like that which Machiavelli and Rousseau recommend, by the following year this permanent potential emergency convinces him that a sovereign dictator is necessary. A commissarial dictator has as his aim the restoration of the constitution, at which point he renders himself redundant and abdicates his position. A sovereign dictator is permanent.

An absolute sovereign is the antidote to the liberal democratic incapacity to confront the political as the fundamental distinction between friend and enemy, the incapacity to decide who the enemy is. Because this capacity, when not norm-governed, is originary, the sovereign activity of deciding reflects Schmitt's view that all political concepts have their origin in theological concepts. What is *ex nihilo* other than God, the unmoved mover?

---

[61] Carl Schmitt, *The Concept of the Political,* p. 46.

[62] In *Die Diktatur,* Schmitt draws a distinction between a commissarial dictatorship and a sovereign dictatorship. The former has as its ruling force the restoration of the constitution through the resolution of a specific crisis. The latter stands in place of a constitution as constant sovereign. This is the sovereign subtly advocated in his *Political Theology* a year later. For an interesting discussion of this shift, see John McCormick, *Carl Schmitt's Critique of Liberalism,* ch. 3.

[63] Schmitt, *Die Diktatur,* p. xviiff.

In this vein, it is critical to recognize that Schmitt does not allow that the sovereign dictator acts with an ethical goal in mind. No ideology or doctrine should guide his actions. Political matters, the province of the sovereign dictator, "can neither be decided by a previously determined general norm nor by the judgment of a disinterested and therefore neutral third party" because matters that are political are autonomous with respect to *any* norms or distinctions.[64] "The decision frees itself from all normative ties and becomes in the true sense absolute."[65]

Indeed, the idea that one might engage in a struggle to the death for any normative value or idea is anathema for Schmitt. He says "all this has no normative meaning, but an existential meaning only . . . There exists no rational purpose, no norm no matter how true, no program no matter how exemplary, no social ideal no matter how beautiful, no legitimacy nor legality which could justify men in killing each other . . . If such physical destruction of human life is not motivated by an existential threat to one's own way of life, then it cannot be justified."[66] It is only by taking him seriously on this point that we can fully appreciate the nature of his exceptionalism and the contrast it presents to republican exceptionalism. The political decision, whose protagonist is the sovereign dictator, cannot be made in accordance with any further norms, or else it ceases to be a political decision. The nature of the decision is and must be existential. Hence, the Schmittian sovereign dictator cannot be understood as a figure who weighs and balances competing norms or as someone who acts with the aim of preserving some ideal of furthering some beautiful goal. The sovereign dictator is godlike in the sense that he is above norms. But, unlike a theological sovereign, to the *extent* that he is political he is not the 'source' of norms either. His is an anomic condition.

The miraculous parallel of the decision corresponds to an understanding of the world that is more broadly chaotic and mystical and where, insofar as God works in mysterious ways, we must predict unpredictability. If politics and human affairs are chaotic then it follows that the mode of managing politics and human affairs must be equally

---

[64] Schmitt, *The Concept of the Political*, p. 27.
[65] Schmitt, *Political Theory*, p. 12.
[66] Schmitt, *The Concept of the Political*, p. 49.

flexible and similarly free of legal and normative constriction. Schmitt's logic is the logic of decisionism.

It is over this question of miracles and mechanism that Schmitt eventually comes to quarrel with Thomas Hobbes, to whom we now turn. Hobbes attempts to marry some degree of empirical mechanism with decisionism, and he thereby unintentionally subverts its logic. Schmitt's critique of Hobbes thus shows the extent to which the assumptions and conclusions, the logic of decisionism, excludes norms.

HOBBES

For Hobbes, no less than for Machiavelli and Schmitt, emergency is the natural state of human political interaction. While the presence of an absolute sovereign goes a long way to offset the chaotic tendencies of humanity, contrary to republican exceptionalists, the institution of the state does not transform humanity. If it were otherwise, Hobbes could not employ the example of our still locked chests and still bolted doors *within* a state to illustrate the human condition outside the state.[67] Hence, here also, emergency is a permanent possibility and the sovereign is not a complete or transformative answer to the human tumult.

Hobbes follows the logic of decisionism in conceiving of absolute government as entailed by permanent potential emergency. From human equality of wants and human equality of capacity Hobbes deduces trouble. "[I]f any two men desire the same thing, which nevertheless they cannot both enjoy, they become enemies; and . . . endeavour to destroy or subdue one another."[68] The logical response to such a condition, according to Hobbes, is to attempt to preemptively master all those who might pose some threat to one's ambitions. Through competition, diffidence, and desire for glory, "it is manifest, that during the time men live without a common Power to keep them all in awe, they are in that condition which is called Warre; and such a warre, as is of every man, against every man."[69] In such a condition, there is no such thing as justice and injustice, which, as positive concepts derived from

---

[67] Thomas Hobbes, *Leviathan*, ch. 13, p. 97. Hobbes citations will refer to chapter as well as page numbers for the ease of those using a different edition.
[68] Thomas Hobbes, *Leviathan*, ch. 13, p. 95.
[69] Thomas Hobbes, *Leviathan*, ch. 13, p. 96.

natural law, are made possible only when positive law is possible, i.e., within a commonwealth. In other words, the state of nature, which is arguably a state of emergency, is an amoral state where norms are suspended or are not yet actual. The state is a necessary condition for the possibility of positive human endeavor because it is only within a state that men need not defend their lives at every moment.

Hobbes holds that men covenant (at least hypothetically) to restrain themselves from their natural designs and desires in order that each be protected from the like designs and desires of others. To this end, they

confer all their power and strength on one Man, or upon one Assembly of men, that may reduce all their Wills, by plurality of voices, unto one Will ... and every one to owne and acknowledge himselfe to be Author of whatsoever he that so beareth their Person, shall Act, or cause to be Acted, in those things which concerne the Common Peace and Safetie, and therein to submit their Wills, every one to his Will, and their Judgements to his Judgement.[70]

Thereby, each transfers all of his rights to a sovereign individual or assembly, and in this way, the human condition, which is a condition of emergency, is held in abeyance even if it is not overcome.

Without quick and decisive action subject to few, if any, concrete constraints, Hobbes can see no peace. It is in this way that Hobbes arrives at the necessity of his absolute sovereign who is beyond appeal and beyond question. His decisionism, like Schmitt's, stems from chaos and unpredictability and flourishes in sovereignty and absolute power.

That this sovereignty be absolute and unquestionable is both logically and practically necessary, Hobbes argues (however unconvincingly) in three ways. First, because we transfer our authority to the sovereign when we contract, we are the author of all the sovereign's actions. We cannot find fault with actions we ourselves have authored. Second, one cannot justify civil disobedience against a remiss sovereign by appealing to higher law or a higher power because one cannot covenant with God unless there is some mediating figure to personate God, such as Moses or a prophet, whose appearances in Hobbes's day, and ours, have been limited. Third, the sovereign cannot be held to be in breach of a contract with his subjects because he is not a party to the contract, which exists

---

[70] Thomas Hobbes, *Leviathan*, ch. 17, p. 131.

between the subjects, not between them (as yet unpersonated as they are) and the sovereign. Moreover, it would be impossible for the sovereign to be a party to the contract without some higher mechanism of enforcement. 'Words without the sword' are as nothing for Hobbes, and so a contract, without a sovereign to enforce it, is as nothing.

In order to keep the peace, only one perspective can be admissible in cases of conflict. The sovereign is

to be Judge both of the meanes of Peace and Defence; and also ... to do whatsoever he shall think necessary to be done ... for the preserving of Peace and Security, by prevention of Discord at home, and Hostility from abroad, and, when Peace and Security are lost, for the recovery of the same.[71]

The sovereign may commit iniquity but never injustice, and the range of liberties the subjects enjoy are determined by the silence of the sovereign's laws.

It is thus absurd to suggest that the sovereign could be called to account for his actions. He is not required to justify them on the basis of any principles or according to any norms. While he ought to obey the 'Natural Lawes,' which Hobbes sets out, he is not bound to do so. For Hobbes, as for Schmitt, the sovereign is outside the bounds of norms and of quotidian ethics, and it is his decision and his alone that constitutes a threat to the polity.[72] Hobbes's sovereign, then, no less than Schmitt's, is a decisionist figure, and this decisionism responds specifically to what are clearly conditions of an emergency or existential nature.

Nonetheless, there are consequential differences to which Schmitt, despite his admiration for Hobbes, devoted an entire book, *The Leviathan in the State Theory of Thomas Hobbes: Meaning and Failure of a Political Symbol.*[73] These differences stem primarily from the different epistemologies employed by each. Hobbes is taken by the new

---

[71] Thomas Hobbes, *Leviathan*, ch. 18, p. 136.

[72] For an account that emphasizes the normless character of Hobbes's sovereigns' decisions, which, nonetheless, does not employ the term decisionism, see Robert Kraynack, "Hobbes' Behemoth and the Argument for Absolutism." Kraynack argues that it is this very normlessness of the sovereign's decisions that separates Hobbes's doctrine from totalitarianism. Regimes of the latter kind claim 'truth' for their corrupt normativism.

[73] Carl Schmitt, *The Leviathan in the State Theory of Thomas Hobbes: Meaning and Failure of a Political Symbol.*

science. Geometry serves as the model of truth-seeking, as it does for so many of Hobbes's contemporaries, and individual reason takes the place of Aristotle as the source of authority.[74] Hobbes joins many of his contemporaries in condemning the continuing dominance of Aristotle in the universities in place of one's own mind in finding what is true.[75] Not long before Hobbes went up to Oxford, the study of authors critical of Aristotle was actually forbidden by decree.[76] Instead, Hobbes advocated the study of geometry as a bridge to the study of logic, necessary, in turn, to considering matters philosophical, religious, and scientific autonomously.[77] Hence, he begins his treatise with definitions, supplements these with premises derived from what he considers to be universal experience, and employs reason to deduce what follows. Hobbes is a modern through and through.

This maintenance of political absolutism, despite the introduction of intellectual individualism, is what gets him into trouble. If one believes that science and geometry are means to truth, and in the rationality of humans generally, then each individual has the capacity to be intellectually autonomous. One of the upshots of intellectual self-government is that one's private reason and belief come to be beyond the reach of the state. What one says and what one does are the purview of the sovereign, but what one thinks or believes is according to individual reason, and over this the sovereign has no control.

Hence arises Schmitt's dispute with Hobbes on the subject of miracles. Hobbes devotes a large section of his *Leviathan* to an extensive critique of the political and intellectual authority of religion and religious leaders, an authority that for Hobbes lacks any justification. In Hobbes's time, miracles are both central features of the legitimization of political power, and, to the extent they serve as evidence of

---

[74] For good discussions of Hobbes's ideas about science and mathematics and their relationship to his thought more generally, see Sorrel (ed.), *The Cambridge Companion to Hobbes*.

[75] "[It] is another Errour of Aristotle's Politiques, that in a wel ordered Common-wealth, not Men should govern, but the Laws. What man that has his naturall Senses, though he can neither write nor read, does not find himself governed by them he fears, and believes can kill or hurt him when he obeyeth not?" Hobbes, *Leviathan*, ch. 46, p. 699.

[76] Sorrel, "A Summary Biography of Hobbes," in *The Cambridge Companion to Hobbes*, p. 17.

[77] Sorrel, "A Summary Biography of Hobbes," in *The Cambridge Companion to Hobbes*, p. 16.

religious authenticity, one source of the religious schisms that wreaked havoc throughout seventeenth century Europe. Hobbes says:

A private man has always the liberty (because his thought is free,) to believe, or not believe in his heart, those acts that have been given out for Miracles ... But when it comes to confession of faith, the Private Reason must submit to the Publique; that is to say, to Gods Lieutenant [i.e., the sovereign]."[78]

Although: "it is lawfull now for the Soveraign to punish any man that shall oppose his Private Spirit against the Laws ... [and] none but the Soveraign in a Christian Common-wealth, can take notice what is, or what is not the Word of God."[79]

While in other respects Hobbes is clearly a decisionist, this is a significant departure from the logic of decisionism. The natural world, which for other decisionists is evidence of theological power and mystery, is not inscrutable for Hobbes. Rather, it is legible for the open-eyed and those who use their reason. The world is not enchanted. Good sense allows us to see that miracles are no longer a live currency and it is through a lack of knowledge or want of reason that people believe in them. Though the world is chaotic, it is ultimately knowable. Because of these epistemological foundations, Hobbes's work is inconsistent with the logic that supports decisionist absolutism.

Decisionism means a rejection of norms in the face of chaos. Hobbes says that men rule, not laws; no one fears paper or words, only swords and men. Schmitt implies in his critique that this is not enough. The religious power of symbols, the fear of God and of demons are essential to political rule. Hobbes deprives the Leviathan of its primeval and mystical power to engender terror, and he thereby deprives the sovereign of the force of the miraculous and the mysterious. The Leviathan, Schmitt tells us, is a mysterious and terrifying creature "garbed, during the course of many centuries in mythical, theological, and cabbalistic meanings."[80] But to the extent that individuals can choose to evaluate the authenticity of the mysterious or miraculous themselves, which is the extent to which

---

[78] Hobbes, *Leviathan*, ch. 38, p. 478.
[79] Hobbes, *Leviathan*, ch. 40, p. 501.
[80] Schmitt, *The Leviathan in the State Theory of Thomas Hobbes*, p. 6.

the world is knowable by individual reason, the Leviathan is deflated, transformed from a mystical and powerful religious force into something mundane, a technical means. The Leviathan is a 'new God,' but this new God is only a huge machine.[81] Hobbes has missed the central importance of the stupefying force of irrational fear. By stripping the sovereign of his essentially mysterious nature he strips him of his power.

Hobbes has thus introduced "the revolutionary, state-destroying distinction between politics and religion"[82] and between public and private reason. It strikes Schmitt as entirely contradictory and nonsensical that individuals are allowed to decide in their hearts the authenticity of miracles so long as their outward words and deeds are consistent with the sovereign's will. This crack, as Schmitt calls it, between public and private reason enables a degeneration and degradation of the sovereign, who, ironically, himself becomes a symbol drained of meaning. The strength with which Hobbes wishes to endow his sovereign is impossible on the terms he sets.[83] Religion and politics cannot be separated and sovereignty and decision constitute the bridge between the two. The turn toward the silent inner, which Hobbes enables and Schmitt sees as distinctively connected to religious matters, constitutes a fissure. A secular, scientific decisionism is not possible.

Certainly intellectual autonomy has often led to political autonomy. Hobbes opened a schism that renders decisionism impossible. To the extent that decisionism and intellectual control entail each other, decisionism seems a dubious doctrine for liberal democrats to contemplate adapting. It is inherently absolutist. Moreover, to the extent that we hold intellectual control to be something of an impossibility, we might question the very coherence of decisionism as a response to emergency.

EXCEPTIONALISM AND THE PROBLEM OF EMERGENCY POWERS

Exceptionalists centralize emergency. Schmitt has described this habit of making emergency an organizing principle of politics as an

---

[81] Schmitt, *The Leviathan in the State Theory of Thomas Hobbes*, pp. 31, 35.

[82] Schmitt, *The Leviathan in the State Theory of Thomas Hobbes*, p. 10.

[83] Yet, "it is possible that behind the image of the Leviathan is hidden a deeper, symbolic meaning. Like all the great thinkers of his times, Hobbes had a taste for esoteric cover-ups." Schmitt, *The Leviathan in the State Theory of Thomas Hobbes*, p. 26.

acknowledgement that the relationship between obedience and protection is at politics' heart.[84] The centrality of protection emphasizes the centrality of danger; and danger is at the core of decisionism. When the aim of political community is conceived as protection, and when that protection is conceived as impossible without unity and force, then obedience is its natural counterpart.

But decisionists exaggerate the chaos and cruelty of human existence at least in a regime already accustomed to rights and the rule of law. Many, from Rousseau to Rawls, have noted that gentle regimes characterized by just principles affect the character of their inhabitants. We might not, with Rawls, expect human character to alter to the point where injustice is no longer to be expected.[85] And we might hope that human character would escape the claustrophobia of a state made up of Émiles and Sophies.[86] But we might nonetheless agree that the more just and better structured the state, the less chaotic and disordered it will be. Emergency, in the sense of an urgent and large-scale threat to order, is common but not constant.

Hence, we should contest the centrality of emergency in the exceptionalist conceptualization of politics. Certainly danger is a common element of political life, and obedience and protection are elements of *any* regime. But, why should danger, why should emergency be *the* central element? Schmitt might answer that whatever is concerned with existence itself must necessarily be that which is most fundamental.[87] Some liberals might reply that, on the contrary, some ideals are worth dying for.

If emergency and danger are not the central elements of political life, neither are they unknown. Though emergency is rarely the constant condition of liberal democracies,[88] it is nonetheless common. There are still emergencies. Does temporary emergency necessitate a temporary

---

[84] In the political theology of another decisionist, Joseph de Maistre, this connection goes so far as to fuse obedience and protection in the guise of providence. We are obedient to providence, and it brings to us what ought to be brought, whether or not this manifests as physical protection. See, for instance, Joseph de Maistre, *Considerations on France*, p. 28.

[85] John Rawls, *A Theory of Justice*, p. 245.

[86] Sophie is, in Rousseau's scheme, to be Émile's ideal companion.

[87] Schmitt, *The Concept of the Political*, p. 49.

[88] I say rarely because there are states, such as Northern Ireland, Israel, and Egypt, that have been under indefinite and lengthy states of emergency.

absolutism? If absolutism follows logically from danger, must accountability be rendered impossible and exceptionalism prove the rule? On the one hand, exceptionalist logic is flawed and its conclusions dangerous. But on the other, we can take from exceptionalism a powerful challenge to the idea that law can rule on its own. The idea of order and its normal or exceptional functioning corresponds to a conflict between the idea of political order as a mechanism which, once set going, runs itself. But we know that the machine is flawed, and hence that it must be run and maintained by someone (by God, by the sovereign, by Jean-Jacques the tutor, by the Prince).

Engaging these historical texts has illustrated the dangers of accepting the norm/exception dichotomy, making us prone to accept an unlimited, unaccountable, and therefore unacceptable authority. Wherever a thinker or political leader asserts the existence of a temporal norm/exception conception of emergencies, a latent assumption of a permanent two-tier ethics necessarily follows. Hence, emergencies that are conceptualized as states of exception *necessarily* come to appear as permanent and permanently exempted from oversight. This inquiry shows the extent of the danger inherent in the everyday norm/exception conception. While we cannot do away with emergencies, we can do away with this deeply flawed conceptual framework. Yet this discourse continues to color legal and political work on emergencies. For example, Ferejohn and Pasquino have argued that differentiating normalcy and exception is critical for safety.[89] But if our eventual concern is the design and implementation of safer emergency powers, it is misguided to draw an ontological distinction between normalcy and emergency while defining emergency as exceptional and emergency powers as beyond the law. We thereby imply emergency might be removed entirely from the purview of rights and other legal and moral norms.

We can avoid the horns of this dilemma by coming to recognize the strong continuities between emergency and everyday relationships between order and justice. These continuities work in both directions. Emergency has rarely been lawless. It has long been embedded within its own codified or common law regimes of rights and moral norms. Necessity does indeed know law. Furthermore, rights derogations have

---

[89] Ferejohn and Pasquino, "The Law of Exception," p. 221.

never been confined to emergencies. The criminal law, for example, is a codified regime of rights derogations in the service of order. We systematically violate rights in the service of order every day. As legal and political scholars contemplate the design and development of new legal and constitutional emergency frameworks, it is critical that we not lose sight of these important continuities. For, to assume that norms and exceptions are the conceptual structure of emergency powers shifts our focus from the myriad possible means of constraint, and blinds us to the continuing force of other countervailing moral norms. It also ignores or downplays the existence of positive nonderogable rights that, in contemporary legal frameworks such as the International Covenant on Civil and Political Rights, define the ultimate boundaries of acceptable emergency action.

The chapters that follow demonstrate that emergency need not be understood through the lens of exceptionalism. From there we can begin to see the coherence of a liberal democratic approach to emergency that can confront the reality of emergency while navigating the horns of the conceptual dilemma and clarifying what is at stake for those who must face the practical dilemmas of government in times of crisis.

3

Two Concepts of Liberalism

I have suggested that the dilemma of emergency is two-pronged. Emergency at its most extreme threatens, on the one hand, the *essence* of liberal democracy, and on the other, its *existence*. If rights are derogated and powers concentrated, two *essential* features of liberalism are overcome. If not, the state or its citizens may succumb to crisis and chaos. In Chapter 2, I argued that those who see emergency powers as an exception from norms present an effective challenge to liberals along the second prong of the dilemma. Flexibility and force keep a state safe in times of emergency, but the checks and balances and rights guarantees of liberal government seem to preclude these. Diffuse power can prevent an efficient response even when a threat is immediate and deadly. But even with power concentrated, the constant and ubiquitous functioning of liberal norms means a liberal state would be constrained from confronting an emergency effectively. So, liberal states, on this understanding, would not survive the severest emergencies.

The solution that the exceptionalists propose, one that would exempt statesmen from accountability to liberal democratic norms and laws, is not one that we can accept. Political leaders cannot, it seems, be bound by norms, but they cannot make exceptions either. Hence, the problem of protecting the state and its citizens in a crisis remains a live one. Given the exigencies liberal democracies have always faced and will always face, can such a state maintain itself both essentially and practically, not only as liberal democratic but as functional?

This chapter explores the resources of liberal democratic theory for meeting the challenge of emergency without jettisoning liberal values. In taking up the problem of emergency from this perspective it joins historical to contemporary debates.

The argument draws its impetus from the insight that our bias toward understanding emergency in norm/exception terms stems partly from the dominant, Kantian approach to civil rights and political right. While some neo-Kantians, and indeed Kant himself, have recognized the problem of emergency, the rational-deductive epistemology underlying this kind of normative theory makes an engagement with the problem tense and uneasy, and often inconsistent. But an alternative epistemology, which we can find in Locke and in the neo-Lockean strain of liberal ethics, suggests a fruitful direction for inquiry into an alternative approach. The key is to understand institutions as flexible means to principled ends, and not as the conclusions of syllogisms.

In underlining these epistemological differences, what is at stake extends beyond the outcomes that each approach allows, critical as such outcomes might be. Each reflects a broader difference in moral perspectives between what Stuart Hampshire has called "the acclaimed virtues of innocence and the undeniable virtues of experience."[1] Hampshire argues that "Moral theory, trying for rational coherence, has covered over the rift and the tidier picture has become a kind of orthodoxy, even though it contradicts experience."[2] What is the place of experience in ethical life and ethical thought?

The chapter illustrates the roots of the two epistemological strands of liberalism. Having shown the paradox inherent in a pure neo-Kantian approach to political ethics, which the question of emergency makes clear, I turn to an examination of emergency in the political thought of John Locke to show how a different epistemological approach provides the necessary institutional flexibility for a liberal democracy to confront the problem of emergency without making exceptions to liberal democratic values. I develop and justify this normative approach in Chapters 4 and 5.

---

[1] Stuart Hampshire, *Innocence and Experience*, p. 12.
[2] Hampshire, *Innocence and Experience*, p. 12.

PHILOSOPHICAL LIBERALISM AND THE REJECTION OF EXCEPTIONALISM

In Chapter 2 I examined the doctrine of exceptionalism in its republican and decisionist varieties, as represented by Machiavelli and Rousseau, and by Hobbes and Schmitt.[3] That Rousseau and Hobbes are exceptionalists shows that this doctrine is not entirely foreign from our tradition. But since Kant, there has been a strong strain of philosophical liberalism that accepts the norm/exception dichotomy but rejects exceptionalism. In arguing that we *cannot* make exceptions from moral or legal norms, even liberals who hold emergency powers to be unjust speak in norm/exception terms. Robert Nozick provides perhaps the most acute illustration.[4]

Nozick's deontological, neo-Kantian approach to rights is exemplified in his idea of "[s]ide constraints upon action [that] reflect the underlying Kantian principle that individuals are ends and not merely means; they may not be sacrificed or used for the achieving of other ends without their consent. Individuals are inviolable."[5] He argues explicitly that individuals cannot be called upon to "bear some costs that benefit other persons more, for the sake of the overall social good" because "there is no *social entity* with a good that undergoes some sacrifice for its own good. There are only individual people ... [so] using one of these people for the benefit of others, uses him and benefits others. Nothing more."[6] Hence, for Nozick the idea of emergency powers is necessarily one of exceptions to absolute norms.

---

[3] That exceptionalism is still taken seriously is evident from a great deal of contemporary political discourse. For example, it served as the rationale for the decision of the Fourth Circuit Court of Appeals in *Hamdi v. Rumsfeld* that an American citizen could forfeit his rights if captured in battle. Then Attorney-General John Ashcroft called this decision "an important victory, which reaffirms the president's [wartime] authority." U.S. Department of State, "Appeals Court Upholds Detention of 'Enemy Combatant,'" http://usinfo.state.gov/dhr/Archive/2003/Oct/09–771737.html, accessed 22 July 2005. This decision was recently overturned by the Supreme Court in *Hamdi v. Rumsfeld*, 542 U.S. 507 (2004), but exceptionalism got a clear nod in Justice Thomas's dissent.

[4] Robert Nozick, *Anarchy, State, and Utopia*, e.g. pp. 30, 40, 47.

[5] Nozick, *Anarchy, State, and Utopia*, pp. 30–1.

[6] Nozick, *Anarchy, State, and Utopia*, p. 33.

The discomfort that a Nozickian style liberal must experience in the face of emergencies is thus clear. Liberals of this persuasion recognize the possibility of catastrophe with the greatest discomfort.[7] With respect to rights in emergencies, Nozick has this to say in a footnote: "The question of whether these side constraints are absolute, or whether they may be violated in order to avoid catastrophic moral horror, and if the latter, what the resulting structure might look like, is one I hope largely to avoid."[8] And so far from an 'academic' matter, such a view was espoused in the 'real world' almost verbatim in a 2006 decision handed down by the German Constitutional Court. In 2005, the German government timidly passed a law, the *Aviation Security Act*, that would allow the military, on the explicit advice of the government, to shoot down a passenger plane that had clearly been hijacked and transformed into a weapon, in the manner of the September 11 attacks on the World Trade Center. Then German President Horst Köhler allowed the measure, but not without discomfort and widespread public uproar. Four citizens, including three lawyers and a pilot, brought the matter before the Constitutional Court, which declared the law incompatible with the *Grundgesetz* in a decision of February 15, 2006. The Constitutional Court issued a stinging retort claiming that

§ 14.3 of the Aviation Security Act is incompatible with the fundamental right to life and with the guarantee of human dignity to the extent that the use of armed force affects persons on board the aircraft who are not participants in the crime. By the state's using their killing as a means to save others, they are treated as mere objects, which denies them the value that is due to a human being for his or her own sake.[9]

While a high court is and should be bound by its consitution, it should always prompt caution when a *theory* avoids the hard

---

[7] Others who, surprisingly and somewhat inconsistently, are willing to make exceptions for exceptions include Ronald Dworkin, who is an emergency utilitarian, despite himself claiming, in *Taking Rights Seriously* (p. 191), that a catastrophe can trump the trumps that are rights.

[8] Dworkin, *Taking Rights Seriously*, p. 30.

[9] http://www.bundesverfassungsgericht.de/en/press/bvg06-011en.html, accessed 05/2008; Bundesverfassungsgericht, Pressestelle Press release no. 11/2006 of 15 February 2006. Zum Judgment of 15 February 2006 – 1 BvR 357/05 – Authorisation to shoot down aircraft in the *Aviation Security* void.

case.[10] Nozick himself recognizes this: "I tiptoe around these incredibly difficult issues here, noting that [my theory] must resolve them explicitly at some point."[11] And yet it does not.

Nozick's discussion of the absolute character of side constraints, which has contemporary echoes in the popular discourse on the war on terror, yields a state that would be without resources to deal with emergencies. Rights have a deontological character for him, and the state or its citizens considered as a group do not constitute an entity with any entitlements or even an 'existence' that can be threatened. No exceptions can be made to norms and no emergency powers are possible on this norm/exception understanding of emergency.

Now, I have suggested that Nozick is an epistemological neo-Kantian, and this is true not only insofar as he understands rights as absolutes, as side constraints that grow from the Kantian imperative to treat people as ends in themselves. For this perspective is intrinsically related to an aspect of Kantian/neo-Kantian methodology: the contemporary analytic thought experiment is a logical relative of transcendental deduction. Both aim to establish that some antecedent is true by means of establishing its necessity for an already established consequent. In the case of a thought experiment, the aim is to establish a principle by showing that we would assent to what follows from that principle, made clear through the illustration of some extreme situation. Similarly, a transcendental argument establishes the synthetic a priori by establishing what must be true in order for some further claim to be true. In neither case does experience come into play *at this point*.

I want to suggest that it is at this point that engagements with emergency in contemporary liberal discourse are led astray. The methodology and the relevant assumptions about the nature of rights are intrinsically connected. For to the extent that right is an a priori matter, we can assume that institutions can be rigid, made up of offices, and not

---

[10] Nozick (*Anarchy, State, and Utopia*) reiterates his hesitance to confront hard cases when he dodges the question of innocent threats and innocent shields. For some reason, despite the prohibition against using people as means, one may do them serious violence or even kill them if one is threatened oneself. How this does not amount to using them as a means only, and without their consent, is unclear, which presumably explains why Nozick says so little about its justification.

[11] Nozick, *Anarchy, State, and Utopia*, p. 35.

of officers. If we can deduce the content of right, we advocate, a priori, those institutions that embody and reflect that conception of right. Institutions are inflexible on this view, as they must be, since it is this very inflexibility that drives this conception of right.

This is clear in Kant's own account of right in *The Metaphysics of Morals*. As we shall see, while Kant's engagement with the problem of emergency is complex, the tensions and difficulties it exhibits stem from the conformity of the theory of right to this model. It is not that experience has no role to play in Kant's political thought. But the role it plays is ill-placed and insufficient. As a result, emergency suggests antinomies in Kant's metaphysics of morals; it brings Kant to make explicitly contradictory statements: he, like many of his intellectual progeny, is sympathetic to certain emergency powers that his doctrine of right specifically excludes.

KANT ON EMERGENCY

I draw, in this account on Kant's engagement with the emergency problem, primarily from *The Metaphysics of Morals* as the mature statement of Kant's ethics and ethical politics, and one that he considered to be for scholarly rather than popular consumption.[12] Here, Kant separates a Doctrine of Right from a Doctrine of Virtue. The former pertains to law and the latter to ethics. A primary difference between the two is the impetus to conform to duties. We can be coerced to do what is in accordance with right because a hindrance to a hindrance of freedom is right.[13] While it is morally worthy to do what is right simply because it is in accordance with right, it is the fact of coercion that provides the primary impetus for right action, on Kant's account. Right provides external reasons for behaving in accordance with duties. Right can be embodied in law and when law is in accordance with right it is just law.[14] The fundamental principle of right is the maximization of freedom in accordance with the freedom of others, and this principle, according to Kant, is a priori.[15]

---

[12] Kant, *The Metaphysics of Morals*. References are to the Academy Edition pagination.
[13] Kant, *The Metaphysics of Morals*, pp. 231–2.
[14] Kant, *The Metaphysics of Morals*, p. 311.
[15] Kant, *The Metaphysics of Morals*, pp. 230–1.

In contrast to external duties of right, which are physically enforceable, duties of virtue are for duties' sake only, and here we are compelled by the internal force of the moral law. We are autonomous when we give the moral law to ourselves in the form of a maxim for ethical action. And it is respect for this autonomy that grounds respect for the dignity of human rationality. Autonomy is freedom in the guise of self-government stemming from rationality. The centrality of rationality stems both from the means through which we arrive at maxims for self-government and from the end of moral action. We act on that maxim that we determine, rationally, we could will to be a universal law. And because we are capable of such rationality, we act so as to treat people as ends in themselves and never as means only.

It is noteworthy that there are no moral premises in the derivation of legal duties, which are simply those that are required in order for the Universal Principle of Right to obtain: "Any action is *right* if it can coexist with everyone's freedom in accordance with a universal law."[16] And it is only on this principle that laws are justified. Now, while emergency is a matter of law and so of right rather than of virtue, a statesman who acts under emergency circumstances acts both *qua* individual and *qua* statesman. Hence, both right and ethics are of interest here; and a central element, which they both share, is the marginalization of the empirical.

Both duties of right and duties of virtue can be determined a priori, without reliance on empirical and contingent fact.[17] Moral laws "hold as laws only insofar as they can be *seen* to have an a priori basis and to be necessary," and one who hoped to come to knowledge of the moral law or the principles of right in some other fashion "would run the risk of the grossest and most pernicious errors."[18] Empirical knowledge, because uncertain and incomplete, can never yield knowledge of what is right and what is just. "Like the wooden head in Phaedrus' fable, a merely empirical doctrine of right is a head that may be beautiful, but unfortunately it has no brain."[19] Only a priori principles, which we can decipher analytically or deduce transcendentally, can yield the kind of

---

[16] Kant, *The Metaphysics of Morals*, p. 230.
[17] Kant, *Critique of Pure Reason*, Cf., A15/B29, A802/B830, A807/B835, A840/B868.
[18] Kant, *The Metaphysics of Morals*, p. 215.
[19] Kant, *The Metaphysics of Morals*, p. 230. See also p. 312.

knowledge Kant thinks is sufficiently secure to escape skepticism. In the field of ethics, this is all the more critical.

It is not that Kant finds no place for experience in ethical-political thought. In essays like "Theory and Practice" and "Idea for a Universal History with a Cosmopolitan Purpose," he hints at this relationship between the rational and the empirical. For instance, Kant cites the role of experience in the development of the just civil constitution "tested in many affairs of the world."[20] But the form of the just state will not depend on experience. Rather, through experience, we will come to recognize the rationally deduced, best constitution. It is an *Entwicklung* rather than a process of creation and refinement. Kant's descriptions of the relationship between the realm of experience and the realm of reason, here, are as dissatisfying as his description of the relationship between the noumenal and the phenomenal realms.

Kant also wishes to exclude inclination, personal preferences, and personal ties, as well as contingent circumstances, to preclude what we might call moral intuition. Our capacity to judge in the face of sentimentality is likely to go astray. Absolute reliance on reason and the moral law is the best response to the weakness of the human condition. Kant does make a concession to the world of things when he suggests that a metaphysics of morals should be followed up with a moral anthropology, which would explore "the development, spreading, and strengthening of moral principles . . ."[21] But such an anthropology is purely descriptive.[22]

Could a state governed by Kantian right and statesmen who are virtuous Kantians confront the challenge of emergency that Schmitt and the exceptionalists set forth? We might think that they could not. For, emergency is inherently unpredictable and what is unpredictable must be met with flexibility. Flexibility, in turn, makes no sense without an empirical focus. And this is yet more urgent if we recognize the specific violations of duties of right and duties of virtue that emergency power concentration and rights derogations seem to entail. Emergency government requires attention to empirical circumstances, and an alteration of moral modes of action in response to these empirical

---

[20] Kant, "Idea for a Universal History," in *Kant's Political Writings*, p. 47.
[21] Kant, *The Metaphysics of Morals*, p. 217.
[22] On Kant's moral anthropology, see Allen Wood, *Kant's Ethical Thought*.

circumstances. Actions that would be patently unjustifiable absent an emergency, such as commandeering property, seem different in the light of an emergency's urgency and scale.

It would then be natural to assume that Kant rejects the possibility of emergency powers outright; that he would consider such powers to be a perfect example of the clouding of the moral law by a moral judgment subject to inclination and nationalist sentimentality. But emergencies are, for Kant, somehow different. With respect to soldiering and killing, spying and policing, and even with respect to matters of taxation, in emergencies, Kant shows himself to be a proponent of special powers.

In times of war or sedition, Kant's standards for duties of right are significantly relaxed. Police can search a private residence, despite the usual restrictions on such activities.[23] Violations of privacy for the benefit of the state are permissible in times of emergency and the police may assume guilt with evidence to follow. What we now call rights of due process Kant happily restricts. Furthermore, Kant is in general fairly permissive with the lives of the innocent citizens of other states in times of war. Far from treating these people as ends in themselves, Kant limits what is not permitted to what would prevent sufficient future trust and goodwill to engender peace. Atrocities are forbidden, but that is all. Indeed, Kant appears to subscribe to the principle '*inter arma silent leges*' although he does not think ethics in general are silent.[24] Other states' citizens are means to winning a war or overcoming the emergency, and this causes Kant little concern.

In institutional terms, Kant is no less surprising. He insists that in various matters, "[t]he head of the state must be authorized to judge for himself whether [certain] measures are necessary for the commonwealth's prosperity, which is required to maintain its strength and stability both internally and against external enemies."[25] The head of state is the final judge of restrictions on freedom that he considers necessary for his ultimate purpose, the preservation of the commonwealth. This may require certain restrictions on right, as well as extraordinary

---

[23] Kant, *The Metaphysics of Morals*, p. 325.
[24] Kant, *The Metaphysics of Morals*, p. 347.
[25] Kant, "On the Common Saying: This May Be True in Theory but It Does Not Apply in Practice," in *Kant's Political Writings*, p. 80.

financial or other measures. Among these prerogatives of a head of state, Kant endorses an emergency taxing prerogative, much along the lines of Charles I's controversial Ship Money tax.[26]

The case of taxation is particularly interesting because here Kant states *explicitly* that the executive may act directly contrary to laws deduced from his principle of right. Although Kant insists that, normally, citizens must endorse their own taxation through their deputies,[27] he allows an exception: executive power may "impose an enforced loan ... by the right of majesty."[28] Against this right there is no appeal or counter-right of rebellion, even in the case of tyrannical misuse of this power.[29] There are no checks on the emergency prerogatives of a Kantian executive. Power is concentrated absolutely. This appears to be so even after humans have reached the state of maturity that Kant calls 'enlightened.'[30] Kant endorses Frederick the Great's dictum that his subjects might argue about whatever they like and however much they like, so long as they obey.[31] But it is hard to square these views with Kant's ethical and political thought. He adheres to the Ciceronian maxim *salus populi suprema lex*,[32] despite the tension of that maxim with his ethical theory more generally.

These examples of unusual powers all concern the usual stuff of emergency powers: concentration of power, derogation of rights on what *appears* to be a sort of emergency utilitarian justification. Kant's political thought, if not his purely ethical thought, is capable of confronting emergencies, at least in a tense and ambivalent fashion. So how is it that Kant is able to justify these claims? There are two directions we might explore before concluding that this apparently incongruous political reasoning stems from prejudices or collapses into inconsistency. Kant raises two elements in the *Metaphysics of Morals* that suggest possible explanations: his notion of imperfect duties and his concessions, however limited, to necessity.

---

[26] This case receives further attention in this chapter.

[27] Kant, *The Metaphysics of Morals*, p. 325.

[28] Kant, *The Metaphysics of Morals*, p. 325.

[29] See, e.g., "Perpetual Peace," in *Kant's Political Writings*, p. 126.

[30] Kant, "An Answer to the Question: 'What Is Enlightenment?'" in Reiss (ed.), *Kant's Political Writings*, pp. 54–60.

[31] Kant, "An Answer to the Question: 'What Is Enlightenment?'" p. 59.

[32] Kant, *The Metaphysics of Morals*, p. 318. The maxim is from Cicero, *On the Laws*, III.3.

Kant distinguishes between perfect and imperfect duties. In the *Groundwork for the Metaphysics of Morals* he tells us that imperfect duties admit of exceptions on the basis of inclination while perfect duties do not.[33] The latter are absolute and incontrovertible and in *The Metaphysics of Morals* he adds that one who fails in these duties is culpable. Failure to observe imperfect duties, on the other hand, constitutes a lack of moral worth, but not culpability. Hence, one deserves no praise for conforming with perfect duties – that is just a matter of course.[34]

With imperfect duties, it is in deciding on a means to meet morally obligatory ends that one's inclinations can be taken into account. Charity is one example. Charity is obligatory, but the amount one gives, or whether this comes in the form of voluntary work or financial contribution, can be influenced by personal circumstances. Here we may take account of our own needs in determining how we fulfill this end.

No duty of right, which is to say no just law, can be an imperfect duty.[35] Since conformity with the law is primarily a matter of right, duties to enforce and observe the law must be perfect duties. It follows from this that it is not possible for the rule of law to be mitigated in accordance with proper adherence to the principle of right. Adherence to the law is absolute. If the law says 'Citizens must agree to their taxation,' no emergency prerogative that overrides such a law could be justified on the basis of an imperfect duty.[36]

So, imperfect duties could only account for apparent violations of a statesman's moral duties. But even here, imperfect duties will not do the job. Kant would not classify the kinds of things emergency might require of a statesman – causing death, telling lies – as imperfect duties.[37] Kant makes this explicit in his discussion of the right of necessity in *The Metaphysics of Morals* where he excludes the necessity of saving one's own life as a worthy excuse for taking the life of another,

---

[33] Immanuel Kant, *Groundwork for the Metaphysics of Morals*, p. 421n.

[34] Kant, *The Metaphysics of Morals*, pp. 390–1.

[35] Kant, *The Metaphysics of Morals*, p. 390.

[36] One might object here that Kant's executive is not subject to the law in the first place. Kant makes this claim in order to preserve the sovereignty of the monarch. Perhaps it would have been more consistent to do away with the concept of sovereignty in his scheme. Kant, *The Metaphysics of Morals*, p. 317.

[37] Kant, *The Metaphysics of Morals*, p. 240.

arguing that "there could be no necessity that would make what is wrong conform with the law."[38] The 'right of necessity,' in this case, concerns killing the innocent to save one's own life and Kant has in mind gruesome cases such as that of stranded sailors who eat their crewmate to stay alive. But cases of emergency would seem to fit under this description as well from the perspective of individual decision making. Killing to preserve one's own life cannot be subject to legal coercion, because the worst the law could threaten would be death: and a threat of death is no threat weighed against a certainty of death. But despite the impossibility of legal threat such an act is still abhorrent and contrary to duties of ethics and duties of right. Physical necessity is never an excuse.

But Kant differentiates between physical necessity and moral necessity. Tucked away in a footnote in the essay "On the Common Saying 'This May Be True in Theory but It Does Not Apply in Practice,'" Kant claims that 'moral necessity' may be considered in a case where an absolute duty, such as the preservation of the state, confronts an imperfect duty:

For instance, it might be necessary for a person to betray someone, even if their relationship were that of father and son, in order to preserve the state from catastrophe. This preservation of the state from evil is an absolute duty, while the preservation of the individual is merely a relative duty (i.e., it applies only if he is not guilty of a crime against the state). The first person might denounce the second to the authorities with the utmost unwillingness, compelled only by (moral) necessity.[39]

Infidelity and a violation of duties of filial care might be justified by moral necessity. But this is true only where imperfect duties conflict with perfect ones. Perfect duties, on Kant's view, cannot come into conflict. In *The Metaphysics of Morals*, Kant rejects wholeheartedly the principle that "'it is better for *one* man to die than for an entire people to perish,'" on the grounds that "if justice goes, there is no longer any value in men's living on earth."[40] It seems, then, that the

[38] Kant, *The Metaphysics of Morals*, p. 236.
[39] Kant, "Theory and Practice," in *Kant's Political Writings*, p. 81.
[40] Kant, *The Metaphysics of Morals*, p. 332.

doctrine of necessity, even of moral necessity, provides no grounds for emergency powers in Kant's ethical and political theory.

Consider how much murkier things become when elsewhere Kant claims that justice perishes with the state. For, in the state of nature, there is "no external justice at all" and hence this state is a worse evil than living in the midst of murderers.[41] For this reason, Kant so often argues that it is a categorical imperative to contract to form a state where none exists.[42] While the state is a necessary condition of justice and while its preservation is an absolute duty, no innocent may be sacrificed in order to preserve it because that too would destroy justice. A sovereign might do what he thinks necessary in an emergency, so long as it would not be contradictory for his action to be willed a universal law.[43] But where this could justify the violation of a leader's other perfect duties – which Kant claims is impossible, but which experience suggests is common – it seems a statesman must simply do nothing.

If principles of political ethics are absolute, as they must necessarily be if they are synthetic a priori statements, then they must be absolutely compelling. But if they are absolutely compelling, then it should not be possible to deviate from them because of purely empirical circumstances. If it really is necessary, if it is a priori on Kant's view, that a people tax themselves rather than have taxes imposed on them, then to make an exception for prerogative or 'the right of majesty' seems questionable. Kant leaves room for emergency powers with incredible scope, but *not for a rigorous explanation or defense of such powers*. We should hope that liberal-democratic emergency powers could do better. Perhaps the same brilliant formal rigor Kant employs in his metaphysical and epistemological writings is not appropriate to political ethics.

The problem of emergency in politics remains the source of antinomies. Because experience is excluded from the process of institutional design, it becomes impossible for Kant to consistently advocate emergency powers. This must be so in any theory conceived along the lines of eliminating conflict through the development of synthetic a priori

---

[41] Kant, *The Metaphysics of Morals*, p. 334.

[42] See, for example, Kant, *The Metaphysics of Morals*, p. 312; Kant, "Perpetual Peace," p. 98.

[43] Kant, "Theory and Practice," p. 79ff.

principles governing political life. Ideal theory trips over the exceptional case unless such cases are buried out of sight. And when it trips, it has no conceptual means of righting itself.

Because emergency requires flexibility and a recognition of conflict, it requires that experience enter both into the design of institutions and the administration of law. While all ethics must be rational-deductive to an extent, a pure or predominantly deductive mode of ethical inquiry is inherently unfriendly to the idea of exceptions, offering little in their place but silence or inconsistent and unsubstantiated assertion. Empirical elements sit uncomfortably at the level of institutional design and legal-moral administration, and hence result in antinomies.

AN ALTERNATIVE APPROACH

If we work only from the example of Kant and liberals who draw on his moral epistemology, we should conclude with John McCormick that Schmitt's "criticism that [liberals after Locke] have an inadequate notion of exceptional circumstances and emergency powers" is "in fact quite legitimate."[44] The fact that emergency will persist regardless means this would be a serious charge. But there is a principled reason why some liberals can confront emergency and others cannot. The distinction is related to the diverse epistemological grounds with which a liberal thinker begins.[45] McCormick's charge applies to neo-Kantian liberals, but not to post-Lockean liberals as such. There is no reason, in principle or in fact, that liberalism should be unable to confront emergency.

We might contrast a pragmatic liberalism – alive to the political element of politics, grounded in experience, but committed to liberal values and principles – with this principled, rational deductive liberalism. In the former case, liberal values are a means to the end of a good collective life, defined partly in terms of freedom. Institutional means are ascertained partly through observation, and hence they have

---

[44] John McCormick, *Carl Schmitt's Critique of Liberalism*, p. 149.
[45] On this, see Pasquale Pasquino, "Locke on King's Prerogative." Pasquino cites Erich Kaufmann as the first to draw attention to this important epistemological distinction.

a built-in flexibility. In the latter case, liberal values are deduced, as
when Kant says that the laws:

> are a priori necessary as laws ... they follow of themselves from concepts of
> external Right as such ... its form is the form of a state as such, that is, of *the
> state as Idea*, as it ought to be in accordance with pure principles of Right. This
> Idea serves as a norm (*norma*) for every actual union into a commonwealth
> (hence serves as a norm for its internal constitution).[46]

The aim is not institutions and laws instrumentally conducive to a range
of good and meaningful lives. Rather, just institutions and laws are deduced from principles.

I want now to explore the capacity of this other, pragmatic kind of
liberalism to confront the problem of emergency powers coherently. Its
different epistemological approach suggests that a state founded on
liberal principles might have the requisite flexibility. The best exemplar
of an empirically grounded liberalism, one that is pragmatic in the sense
of being concerned with means as well as ends, is indeed the liberalism of
John Locke. But while Locke is the best exemplar, he is not the only one.
Though many have noted that Locke's liberalism has resources to confront
emergency,[47] I am interested in exploring what it is that makes him and
some later liberals able to confront emergency while other liberals cannot. Locke's pragmatic liberal approach to emergency is echoed in, for
instance, Alexander Hamilton's approach to emergency in *The Federalist
Papers*.[48] It is also very much the view of Thomas Jefferson. President
Jefferson saw the role of the statesman as self-sacrificial. He held that
emergency provisions could trump the laws when the public good
required it. Should he be punished for his actions, so be it. "Every good
officer must be ready to risk himself."[49]

Any liberal with empiricist leanings and an inductive mode of
approaching politics and political ethics is theoretically able to furnish
the resources necessary for confronting the question of emergency.

---

[46] Kant, *The Metaphysics of Morals*, p, 313.
[47] Three recent examples are Pasquino, "Locke on King's Prerogative"; Vicente Medina,
"Locke's Militant Liberalism"; and Clement Fatovic, "Constitutionalism and Contingency: Locke's Theory Of Prerogative."
[48] Alexander Hamilton, James Madison, and John Jay, *The Federalist*, no. 23.
[49] Letter from Jefferson to Claiborne, 3 February 1807, quoted in M. Dennison, "Martial
Law: The Development of a Theory of Emergency Powers, 1776–1861," p. 58.

LOCKE'S LIBERALISM OF EXPERIENCE

John Locke's *Second Treatise on Government* and his *Letter Concerning Toleration* demonstrate arguments for limited government with separated powers, for the fundamental law of liberty and property, and for toleration, freedom of conscience, and the separation of church and state. Hence, given Locke's concern with the limitation of arbitrary government, an emergency power of kings might seem strange.[50] Why, we might reasonably ask, describe checks on royal (or executive) power, and then show means of overcoming them? If the purpose is to limit the King's *Spielraum*, why then release with the left hand what was bound with the right? Locke's instrumental and empirical approach gestures toward the answer: in times of emergency, it is empirically the case that the end of the public good might be better served through different procedures or institutions. Recent work on Locke has aimed at coming to an understanding of the exact function and status of the prerogative power in Locke's constitutional thinking. Such work misses the fundamental insight toward which Locke's work points: institutions are means. And the moral criteria for means include (but are not limited to) effectiveness. Insofar as effectiveness is partly determined by circumstances, changing circumstances require flexible means.

Locke and Kant reach some of the same institutional conclusions, but their different methodologies rest on different epistemologies. And it is this difference that allows Locke squarely and unabashedly to confront the question of emergency in a principled way. In this section, I will describe Locke's engagement with emergency, arguing that his general approach (if not its details) makes possible a flexible liberal response to emergency that emphasizes continuity in principles and accountability. Finally, I will explain how Locke's epistemology *specifically* enables this approach.

Locke joins Machiavelli, Rousseau, and Schmitt in the view that politics and the political landscape are ultimately unpredictable. Because all actual laws are made by actual people, who cannot tell the future, who cannot anticipate what might transpire over the course of time, and who can so much less anticipate what might transpire

---

[50] John Locke, *Second Treatise of Government*, s. 158.

urgently, there must be some flexibility in means of response in the service of the public good, the *salus populi*. Laws cannot anticipate every situation and may occasionally work directly against the public good. The law is a solidification of wisdom and deliberation, partly inductive in nature, about what might be best for the commonwealth *qua* collection of individuals. Hence cases might arise that run contrary to this collected wisdom. The positive law, on this view, is not 'true,' is not deduced purely, but rather approximates the general case. Outliers are to be expected. "[It is] not . . . possible that the first framers of the government should, by any foresight, be so much masters of future events . . . " that no unexpected case might arise.[51] On such occasions, the executive may explicitly break the law. Locke's famous example is that of a row of houses on fire. The executive can order the destruction of a person's home for the purpose of preventing the spread of the conflagration, although this destruction of private property is obviously a clear violation of both positive law and of one manifestation of natural law as Locke conceives of it.

Ultimately, "As much as may be all the members of the society are to be preserved,"[52] and that end is best met through a give and take of positive law and politics. The idea that the public good is a higher law than any positive law finds its lasting formulation in Cicero's dictum, which, as we saw, Kant also claimed to embrace; Locke cites *salus populi suprema lex* as "certainly so just and fundamental a rule that he who sincerely follows it cannot dangerously err."[53] A prerogative, subject to Cicero's dictum, is necessary.

But Locke is well aware of its dangers, too. Even in the exercise of emergency prerogative, the legislature and the people it represents remain fundamentally in control. The legislative power is superior to the executive in general, "for what can give laws to another must needs be superior to him . . . the legislative power must needs be supreme, and all other powers in any members or parts of the society derived from and subordinate to it."[54] So, unless the executive and legislative powers are united – which, given the temptation to exempt oneself from the law,

---

[51] Locke, *Second Treatise of Government*, s. 156. See also s. 159, s. 160.
[52] Locke, *Second Treatise of Government*, s. 159. See also s. 163.
[53] Locke, *Second Treatise of Government*, s. 158.
[54] Locke, *Second Treatise of Government*, s. 150.

Locke considers to be unwise – the former is subservient to the latter. This is true even under emergency circumstances. The legislature has the power "to punish for any mal-administration against the laws."[55] Moreover, if the executive employs its capacity for force in a manner contrary to the aims set for him by the legislature, or, if he obstructs the activities of the legislature, then, Locke explains, it is as though he has entered into a state of war with the people, who may oppose him in any way they see fit. "The use of force without authority always puts him that uses it into a state of war, as the aggressor, and renders him liable to be treated accordingly."[56]

Prerogative is not a possession of princes, a right, but a fiduciary power. Any part of what was once at the prince's discretion may be codified by a legislature. After all, "a rational creature cannot be supposed, when free, to put himself into subjection to another for his own harm – though where he finds a good and a wise ruler, he may not perhaps think it either necessary or useful to set precise bounds to his power in all things . . ."[57] What limits prerogative is politics: the executive's power is checked through subjection to popular will both directly through the implicit right of revolution, the appeal to heaven, and indirectly through the legislature's power to restrain or recall him. Ultimately, the prince must look to his neck, Locke warns.[58]

Locke's understanding of the legislature's role in reining in prerogative doubtless stemmed in part from the vivid illustration provided by the Ship Money scandal.[59] Between 1634 and 1636, King Charles I of England had brought the matter of emergency prerogative to a head through abuse of his prerogative to raise an emergency tax known as Ship Money. Under common law, in times of emergency, monarchs could impose a levy on those counties bordering the sea to be paid in ships and crew, or, in lieu of these, in cash. The custom had long been

---

[55] Locke, *Second Treatise of Government*, s. 153. It is noteworthy that the legislature, in its turn, is subject to a check by the people, should it, like the executive, fail to meet the ends set for it by the people. It is they who author its power.

[56] Locke, *Second Treatise of Government*, s. 155.

[57] Locke, *Second Treatise of Government*, s. 164.

[58] Fatovic has argued that this represents an interesting departure from the modernist element in early liberal thought. For Locke's prerogative is wielded by a specific person and not an office holder.

[59] Here, I primarily follow S. R. Gardiner, *The Personal Government of Charles I: 1628–1642*.

that the king could exercise this prerogative when urgency precluded the time-consuming process of calling Parliament, whose mandate it normally was to provide the king with funds. Charles had not only attempted to raise funds from *all* counties, inland as well as coastal, but had done so when it was unclear that any real urgency prevented Parliament's involvement. In fact, the King was engaged in a series of incompetent political machinations that had little to do with *salus populi*. England was not actually at war, yet Charles had to raise funds to meet obligations he had undertaken to Spain at the expense of the Dutch, even as he was aiding the Flemish at the expense of the Spanish. The obligations of his incompetent bungling had to be accomplished without calling a Parliament, since presumably Parliament's involvement would give evidence of his various intrigues to his enemies. No doubt it would also have been wildly unpopular with his subjects.

Despite the concurrence of a (cowed) judiciary, the move met with increasing resistance from Charles's subjects and their representatives. Did the King's prerogative include the right to decide on his own whether an emergency existed or not?[60] This abuse of power was one factor in Charles I's eventual trial and execution. Locke had, in this case, a recent and graphic historical example of the abuse of emergency prerogative and a legislature's power to address it.

It is interesting to note the transferability of this scheme to a contemporary liberal parliamentary system. Locke's executive, like a cabinet, can do nearly anything he conceives of as beneficial, as furthering the public good. But the prince-executive, like a cabinet-executive, must constantly recognize that his powers are fiduciary. Cabinet must face reelection or a no-confidence vote. In the worst cases of abuse, criminal charges might be laid. The prince may lose his head. While free rein is a dangerous necessity, the informal powers and constraints of politics can make it marginally safer.

Now, one might question whether Locke's appeal to heaven is effective and coherent as an after the fact remedy, a threat to keep prerogative reined in. Why should we assume a united response to uses of prerogative, assuming as that does that the people are of one mind? And if they are not (and surely they are not), then *who* appeals to heaven? The basis for such an objection is Locke's own keen awareness

---

[60] This is a doctrine, as we have seen, to which Kant wholeheartedly subscribed.

of the radical and violent differences that may seize hold of members of the same community, and of the fundamentally insoluble character of these differences. He is clear, for instance, that Christian sects will find little to judge between them:

> Whatsoever any Church believes, it believes to be true; and the Contrary unto those things, it pronounces to be Error. So that the Controversie between these Churches about the Truth of their Doctrines, and the Purity of their Worship, is on both sides equal; nor is there any Judge ... by whose Sentence it can be determined.[61]

The appeal to heaven against a tyrant's rule, against abuses of prerogative and on the grounds of the good of the people, seems tenuous as a result. Different factions may understand the public good radically differently.[62] What the prince does may seem perfectly in line with the *salus populi* dictum to some, and to others may seem the very soul of tyranny. Hobbes and Schmitt will ask: Who decides? Locke can only answer: "God alone. For there is no Judge upon earth between the Supreme Magistrate and the People."[63] Schmitt or Hobbes would argue that this spells disaster if God is not personated by the sovereign. Liberals would note the vulnerability of cultural, religious, and ethnic minorities. This is certainly a serious difficulty, but not an insurmountable one. If the notion of public good is set out in advance, for instance in the form of general principles or values in a constitution, this can go some way toward defining what constitutes the public good for a particular liberal democratic state, so long as there are mechanisms for allowing the constitution to evolve.

The importance of Locke's position comes not from the particular institutions, but from the mode of their design. What distinguishes him from Schmitt or Hobbes is the empirical claim that well-designed institutions, specific to circumstances, may often be sufficient to prevent civil war. It is the recognition of this particular kind of alliance between offices and office holders that separates Locke's prerogative power from the exceptionalism of Schmitt on the one hand and the

---

[61] John Locke, *A Letter Concerning Toleration*, p. 32.
[62] This problem is also discussed by Ian Shapiro in *The Evolution of Rights in Liberal Theory*, p. 116.
[63] Locke, *A Letter Concerning Toleration*, p. 49.

anti-exceptionalism of the neo-Kantian on the other. For one thing, Locke holds that a threat to the liberal state is determinable *by someone* but partly on the basis of rules. This is true both in terms of the decision about who counts as an enemy and in terms of criteria for confronting enemies. For Locke there are rules of war while for Schmitt there are not. One cannot just exterminate enemies, nor can one determine them as enemies wholly subjectively as Schmitt's theory would allow, or even require. "For Schmitt, to be an enemy is to be perceived as such by another who is willing to engage the enemy in mortal combat, while for Locke to be an aggressor is to violate the natural rights of others unjustifiably."[64]

Moreover, because there are criteria for declaring and confronting emergencies it becomes possible to dispense with the absolute character of the executive, even to subject this executive himself to scrutiny on the basis of these criteria. This eventually became a core issue in the Ship Money case. Charles's capacity to decide when there was or was not an emergency was, according to him (as it later would be for Carl Schmitt), the essence of his prerogative. Charles had the *legal* right to claim that emergency existed and danger was imminent, whether or not objectively this was the case. He could call an emergency into existence on his word. If we grant that there is a subjective element to determining whether an emergency exists, the question was whether Charles's legal right might be safer in the hands of a parliamentary cabinet. In Schmittian terms, the question was where sovereignty should lie, if anywhere. And so it is arguably exactly at this point, at the point where criteria and accountability for decisions on the existence of emergency come into question, that true separation of powers is clarified and actualized. So, the importance of Locke's account of the question of emergency criteria and oversight should not be underestimated in terms of its broader ramifications for the history of responsible government.

It is because there are no criteria for emergency or enmity and because there is no higher judge to which earthly creatures can appeal that decisionists like Carl Schmitt have insisted upon the necessarily absolute character of the executive or sovereign. But here, norms of public good and the threat of an appeal to heaven to enforce them allow for

---

[64] Medina, "Locke's Militant Liberalism," p. 353.

limitations on the sovereign's power. In other words, the sovereign is no sovereign but a mere executive with fiduciary powers.

Hence, despite his advocacy of prerogative powers, it is not correct to call Locke an exceptionalist if we mean one who holds that, under special circumstances, norms cease to apply and censure lacks justification. Pasquale Pasquino sees Locke's account in this light. Both prerogative and the right to resist or appeal to heaven show that "the rule of law cannot put [the members of a community's] destiny in their hands."[65] To the extent that the law, at least the positive law, is insufficient, Pasquino holds that Locke is open to the exceptional case. Yet "to be sure," Pasquino says, "it stands very far from any 'absolutist/ decisionist' political theory, on one hand, and from any 'rationalist' hypothesis, on the other."[66]

It is true that, in Locke's argument, the executive may exercise prerogative in the absence of, or even contrary to, positive law. Property may, under certain conditions, be destroyed and people compelled to act. Locke might thus be regarded as a legal exceptionalist. But because the law cements aspects of the same principles (of public good, of natural law in general) that the executive employs to violate it, emergency prerogative is not exercised in the *absence* of norms.

The continuity between normal and exceptional politics is here evident. Because norms continue to govern the use of prerogative and of an appeal to heaven, both with respect to when these may be exercised and with respect to how, the claim that Locke is open to the exceptional case is not strictly correct insofar as it implies exceptionalism. The Lockean executive, whose power is partly free and partly scripted, is to be bound by a principle of concern for the well-being of the individual citizens of the commonwealth, taken together, and this is the same principle that governs everyday ethical-political life. The relevant principles are continuous, not exceptional.

I am not suggesting that we adopt Locke's principles and framework as such. Instead, I want to draw attention to his approach, which seems to provide a direction for circumventing the horns of the norm/exception dichotomy by emphasizing continuity of principle and the instrumentality and partial continuity of institutions. The executive is *always*

---

[65] Pasquino, "Locke on King's Prerogative," p. 205.
[66] Pasquino, "Locke on King's Prerogative," p. 205.

subservient to the legislature, whether or not the executive wields prerogative, whether or not the people appeal to heaven. While the law is not 'true,' is not iron, can be superseded, variants of the same institutional structures and moral norms operate continuously.

Why do Locke's liberal institutions have this flexibility whereas Kant's do not? Locke is famous for his empiricism and for a correlative pragmatism, and I suggested earlier that it was these epistemological underpinnings that are responsible for his more successful confrontation with emergency. This empirical approach, this instrumental understanding of institutions and offices means officers have more flexibility, judgment plays a larger role. Indeed, the officer's capacity for judgment is an intrinsic part of the office itself. There is a recognition of the messiness of human affairs, and of the multiplicity of often conflicting principles that govern them.

In the *Essay Concerning Human Understanding*, Locke tells us that "all the materials of Reason and Knowledge ... [come from] Experience: In that, all our knowledge is founded and from that it ultimately derives itself."[67] His epistemology exhibits a strong continuity with his pragmatic politics, not only through the powerfully egalitarian character of autonomy in acquisition of knowledge,[68] but also in terms of the structure of its arguments. Locke grounds many of his key arguments, political and otherwise, in empirical phenomena. He "appeal[s] to every one's own Observation and Experience."[69] Consider Locke's argument against the claim that moral principles are innate: were it so "we must then find them clearest and most perspicuous, nearest the Fountain, in Children and illiterate People ... Let them take which side they please, *they will certainly find it inconsistent with visible matter of fact, and daily observation.*"[70] It is on the grounds of empirical fact that Locke makes claims on behalf of the empirical grounds of knowledge.

This empiricism, this pragmatic mode of argument, also characterizes much of his political work. In his *Letter Concerning Toleration*,

---

[67] John Locke, *An Essay Concerning Human Understanding*, II.1.2.

[68] Locke, *An Essay Concerning Human Understanding*, II.1.2. In the "Epistle to the Reader" Locke speaks of "he who has raised himself above the Almes-Basket, and not content to live lazily on scraps of begg'd Opinions, set his own Thoughts on work, to find and follow Truth," p. 6ff.

[69] Locke, *An Essay Concerning Human Understanding*, II.1.1.

[70] Locke, *An Essay Concerning Human Understanding*, I.2.20. My italics.

Locke does not argue for the inherent value of toleration, nor does he argue that it is the only principle consistent with respecting some inherent feature of human beings. Instead, he argues largely on the basis of empirical consequences that religion is never a ground for the invasion of civil rights or the abuse of personal property. "Those that are of another Opinion, would do well to consider with themselves how pernicious a Seed of Discord and War, how powerful a provocation to endless Hatreds, Rapines, and Slaughters, they thereby furnish unto Mankind."[71] Locke does not set toleration as an axiom. Nor does he deduce it transcendentally or from more fundamental axioms. Rather, he looks to experience and there finds good reason to set forth a maxim in the strongest terms. The same is true of his discussions of political institutions.

Consider Locke's argument for the separation of executive from legislative power. Men come together because, says Locke, quoting 'the judicious Hooker,'

> we are not by ourselves sufficient to furnish ourselves with competent store of things needful for such a life as our nature doth desire, a life fit for the dignity of man; therefore to supply those defects and imperfections which are in us, as living singly and solely by ourselves, we are naturally induced to seek communion and fellowship with others.[72]

Having come together in community while still in the state of nature, those conflicts that inevitably arise have no mediator. Each can decide his own case, and, empirically, each is likely to be partial to his own case. Violence ensues. These are "inconveniences" characteristic of the state of nature, and, in forming a civil state, we further the Lockean ultimate good of "preserving all mankind."[73] In the civil state, all can appeal to an authority set up for that purpose, and this prevents violence by settling disputes peaceably.[74]

But under an absolute government there is no one to judge between the prince and his "slave" (as Locke calls a subject of an absolute

---

[71] Locke, *A Letter Concerning Toleration*, p. 33.
[72] Locke, *Second Treatise of Government*, s. 21.
[73] Locke, *Second Treatise of Government*, s. 11.
[74] Locke, *Second Treatise of Government*, s. 90.

monarch).[75] In such a condition, not only has the subject no recourse to his own reason, as he would have in the state of nature, he has nowhere else to appeal. This becomes serious because "he that thinks that absolute power purifies men's blood and corrects the baseness of human nature, need read but the history of this, or any other age, to be convinced of the contrary."[76] Here, and in what follows, Locke gives a purely empirical account of why powers ought to be separated: empirically, kings have a poor record of keeping their hands to themselves and judging justly. Because of this fact about the world, in order to reach the principled end of *salus populi*, there must be checks and balances, some right of appeal, to keep kings trustworthy. The separation of powers is prudent as much as it is rational.

Institutions are instrumental. What serve as instantiations of ends in the philosophy of Kant are means for Locke. To the extent that there are cases where institutions work against their own principled purpose, Locke's liberalism of experience provides means of overriding them for the sake of this same purpose.

It is important to keep in mind that while the institutions Locke recommends are justified on the basis of their instrumental value, this does not entail that Locke's ethics must ultimately be utilitarian.[77] For, some might object that the advantage of the Kantian approach is that it respects rights (qua institutions) in a way that a utilitarian approach does not. On one hand, even the most deontological approach to ethics looks to the effects of action. How else, for instance, could we know if we could will a maxim to be a universal law? But on the other, Locke is not strictly a utilitarian. He invited this charge because he claimed that morality was as demonstrably true as mathematics without ever offering a sound demonstration. This "caused him much subsequent distress as one friend or enemy after another inquired insistently about his progress towards carrying out the demonstration."[78] As a result, Locke's

---

[75] Locke, *Second Treatise of Government*, s. 91.

[76] Locke, *Second Treatise of Government*, s. 92.

[77] Nonetheless, Locke has often been cited as one of the forerunners of British utilitarianism. See for instance, John Dunn, *Locke*, p. 82.

[78] See Dunn, *Locke*, p. 72. Locke's arguments are found in Bk 4, ch. 4, of the *Essay Concerning Human Understanding*. There, at s. 7, he says "moral knowledge is as capable of real Certainty as Mathematicks." For an instructive discussion of these arguments and their failures, see Nicholas Jolley, *Locke: His Philosophical Thought*, p. 178ff.

moral claims, political and otherwise, are notoriously contentious.[79] But the conclusion of the natural law theorist Heinrich Rommen rings true: "Locke's empiricism in epistemology undermine[d] the philosophical bases of the natural law ... [but] Locke ... contented himself with a belief in natural law as a dictate of common sense."[80] Locke simply 'knows' that the laws of nature are true, even if his attempts to show this often fail. He, like generations of meta-ethicists after him, began from the *assumption* that such principles must be true, and set about attempting to justify them post facto. And however often he fails to demonstrate the soundness of morality with the certainty of mathematics, it will convince him only of his own failing, and not that morality, in fact, is unfounded. How many among us are different? Even Kant began in this way.

Locke holds the principles of natural law, and particularly the *salus populi suprema lex*, to be sure and ultimate. Although he is foggy on the question of duties that are correlative to rights,[81] there is no reason in principle why such solid moral principles are incompatible with a certain pragmatism, with a perspective that looks to empirical knowledge to determine the most effective means of fulfilling duties or of achieving ends. Whether or not this is in fact the way that Locke argues (and I think it is at least related), here is how this might be done.

A POLITICAL ETHICS OF EXPERIENCE

Strictly speaking, a deontologist holds that the right comes before the good. Duties outweigh ends. But duties and ends are often related and this is particularly true in political life. It is a statesman's and a legislator's duty, on Locke's view, to preserve the people's welfare. Here is

---

[79] Leo Strauss suggested that Locke intentionally but quietly pulls the rug out from under moral certainty. See *Natural Right and History*, p. 202ff. Michael Zuckert makes the related claim that Locke leads readers to conclusions consistent with his *actual* views about natural law, while concealing his subversive premises. See *Natural Rights and the New Republicanism*, p. 288. Interpreters like Dunn, Pocock, and Tully, on the other hand, find in Locke a robust theism that ultimately grounds his moral claims, even if Locke is sometimes inconsistent.

[80] Heinrich A. Rommen, *The Natural Law: A Study in Legal and Social History and Philosophy*, p. 90.

[81] See the discussion in Shapiro, *The Evolution of Rights in Liberal Theory*, p. 101, p. 124ff.

where empirical considerations might come into play. Consider Kant's idea of imperfect duties, for example, the duty to be charitable. There may well be a large number of means of fulfilling this duty, and Kant thinks that it is acceptable in this case to exercise flexibility with regard to means. Personal preferences might come into play, according to Kant, and arguably, here, one preference might relate to one's ends in fulfilling this duty. Charity can serve many purposes after all. One may have a preference for relieving suffering caused by illness, or else by poverty. One may prefer to support the cultivation of excellence in the arts or in scholarship. Once such a preference has been determined, it is an empirical matter how best to fulfill the duty of being charitable, through most effectively alleviating suffering or supporting excellence, and so on. 'Best' here describes criteria of efficiency and effectiveness, taking careful account of other duties. I call this claim, that moral ends necessitate the best moral means, the 'most moral means principle' and we will revisit it. How one chooses to execute one's duty to be charitable is thus related to empirical considerations and to ends. Pragmatism through empiricism, an ethics of ends, and an ethics of duties are not mutually exclusive.

The same is true of many of the duties that Kant considered perfect. We might think of institutions as the means of getting from the political leader's duty to "preserve and further the good of the people" to an end where this obtains. Depending on empirical conditions, there may be multiple means of fulfilling this duty. Locke thinks this is so, and it is for this reason and in this way that pragmatism and empiricism provide Locke with a means of describing institutions with the flexibility to confront emergency.

The trouble comes in confusing the institutions with the values the institutions are intended to further.[82] Here, one presumes from the outset that the institutions are themselves inherently valuable, as opposed to the ends the institutions are designed to pursue.[83] This is like confusing "Everyone has the duty to give 2 percent of their income to the United Way each year" with "Be charitable." Locke proposes

---

[82] Jolley makes a related claim about Locke's ethics in *Locke*, p. 182.

[83] I do not mean to suggest that institutions cannot take on an inherent value through custom, familiarity, and tradition, just as one might prefer the extra inconvenience and expense of living in an old house, because one's family has occupied it for a century, to moving to a newly constructed condominium.

institutions, which, on the basis of empirical knowledge, would be the most effective in fulfilling duties.

Locke's liberalism and his prerogative power of kings are instructive. The law is not a machine, for Locke, not the conclusion of a syllogism.[84] His is a political ethics of experience and agency that recognizes the complex interplay of principles and force. Allowing high-level principles like *salus populi* to transform into action based on experience makes ethics more practical. This is a good thing given that, fundamentally, ethics are for guiding action, not just for the amusement of philosophers.

We can now begin to see how Locke's empirical liberalism provides a direction for escaping from the norm/exception dichotomy's grip. Insofar as he shows how a government of men and a government of laws are not mutually exclusive, a government of men need not be *exceptional* government. This provides a middle way between the exceptionalists' insistence that the world is too unpredictable to be governed by laws and the philosophical liberals' insistence that only laws can govern. It provides a direction for inquiring how emergency action might be justified, even while norms remain in force. That institutions might be largely (or originally) of instrumental value seems like a promising direction for thinking about the question of the rule of law in emergencies.

CONCLUSION

We began with the challenge that emergency poses to the continued existence of the liberal democratic state in a functional form. Carl Schmitt and others have charged that neutrality, separation of powers, and obsession with positive norms render liberalism incapable of meeting the challenge of emergency. Although, as we have seen, neo-Kantian philosophical liberalism is open to Schmitt's charge, I have argued that grounding liberal institutions in empirical considerations

---

[84] Pasquino, noting this mixture of empirical and rational in Locke's mode of proceeding, remarks that rather, the executive "is endowed with its own will and responsibility that permit it to face the unpredictable." See "Locke on King's Prerogative," p. 202. And John Dunn also concludes that, ultimately, Locke is not a constitutional but a political thinker who "set human good intentions above constitutional rigour." See *The Political Thought of John Locke*, p. 122.

can provide the necessary means of confronting the reality of emergency within the purview of a liberal democratic framework.

Where Kant's liberalism was the embodiment of the truth of right, Locke's commitment to liberal institutional principles has its origins, and remains firmly anchored in the empirical realities of politics. Because Locke's institutions (as opposed to the values they are meant to further and protect) are derived in part from experience, and because they are partially inductive in nature, his liberalism has the *epistemological* resources to begin to confront the problem of emergency. It is specifically because this kind of liberalism does not reduce the problem of emergency to one of norms and exceptions that it is able to escape the dilemma. It does so by conceiving of institutions and laws differently. By conceding that there is something, which we might call agency, that stands between the law and its application, we create room for an emergency politics that is effective, but without the suspension of norms. Insofar as this is true of the functioning of laws and institutions always, and not simply in times of emergency, the continuity becomes yet clearer.

The idea of a liberalism of experience that can confront emergency is not a clear and open road to safety. It is a glimpse of a path through dark woods. Many dangers remain on either side. But, because, as Stuart Hampshire has suggested, the identification of "morality with innocence . . . would ultimately set the politicians free to disregard morality altogether," it is a path worth exploring further.[85] The next two chapters take up this task.

[85] Hampshire, *Innocence and Experience*, p. 12.

4

Are Rights Derogations Always Wrong?

Because no state can long survive if liberal values function to the exclusion of all others, states derogate rights. Nonetheless, for some, rights derogations are "a kind of blasphemy against our deepest moral commitments . . . even in a supreme emergency."[1] This chapter confronts the paradox of a necessary blasphemy. Drawing on the conclusions of the previous chapters – the dangers of exceptionalism and the possibilities inherent in a liberalism of experience – it presents a moral framework for managing this dilemma. I will argue that emergency rights derogations do not constitute exceptions from liberal democratic values, but are instead the manifestation of countervailing existential values, and in particular the value of order. Liberal values most visibly govern the day-to-day functioning of states, but states are made possible by existential ethics that relate to order. When a state is threatened its capacity to maintain order is threatened also, but because this ordering function has a moral character intrinsically connected to the rights and civil liberties it derogates, we have a second order obligation to preserve the state's capacity to fulfill its function. A liberal democratic order has no content or actuality without rights or the moral information they carry, and rights have no actuality without order. Hence, order is not a special concern in times of emergency, it functions as a value beyond these *exceptional* circumstances. The ethics governing the preservation of order are not exceptional but constant.

---

[1] Michael Walzer, *Just and Unjust Wars*, p. 262. Parentheses removed.

The limitation of rights when they conflict with each other or with further values is a constant element of political life also.

It follows from this that the necessity of preserving the state in no way eclipses liberal political obligations. For, if the preservation of the state, however less urgent, is a daily concern, and order is an everyday value, then if liberal political obligations obtain day to day, we would require some special reason why they should cease to obtain under emergency circumstances. If enforcing and upholding order can coexist with rights everyday, these varying kinds of values can coexist in emergencies too. This model can maintain a commitment to rights even as it confronts the necessity of emergency powers. Deliberation can mediate those conflicts that arise in practice. This model is safer and more faithful to the phenomena than are exceptionalist or neo-Kantian liberal approaches to emergency. It shows how liberal democracies with good emergency powers might remain liberal democratic, but it also provides insight into ethical politics in general.

It is not my intention to suggest that the framework that unfolds over the next two chapters binds all the loose ends and gives all the right answers. Indeed, I mean to suggest quite the opposite. Political ethics are irreducibly complex and the problems they help us navigate are often permanent and tragic ones. No moral framework could render emergencies and emergency powers perfectly safe, nor could such a framework simply reveal the right course of action. But, in what follows, I clarify the terms of the dilemma in such a way that, thereafter, moral debate, action, and judgment can be clearer, more effective, more accurate, and more trenchant. This in turn can make emergency powers a little safer.

After drawing out some conceptual and ethical problems with the norm/exception perspective, I present arguments justifying the possibility of emergency rights derogations in liberal democracies. I show how this ethical framework is conceptually and ethically superior to a framework based on the norm/exception dichotomy, and what ramifications the argument might have for our understanding of liberalism in general.

THE TROUBLE WITH NORMS AND EXCEPTIONS

We have seen that thinkers have historically relied on a dichotomy between norms and exceptions to show both the immorality and the amorality of emergency powers. In Chapter 2 I explored the idea of exceptionalism in both its republican and its decisionist guises. I argued that, on the whole, the presuppositions and methodology of the exceptionalist perspective render it fundamentally unhelpful because it negates the possibility of accountability. Accountability is, after all, fundamentally reliant on norms that serve as criteria. In Chapter 3 I showed how neo-Kantian liberals rely equally on this norm/exception dichotomy, which excludes the possibility of a fruitful confrontation with emergency. Neither of these perspectives is satisfactory. Indeed, thinking about emergency in terms of norms and exceptions in the first place is conceptually and normatively confused. Conceptual problems include slippage between descriptive and normative senses of exception and correlative problems surrounding the concept of necessity, which is often used as an explanation for exceptionalism. Normative problems reflect the tensions involved in failing to acknowledge the reality of moral conflict or turning ethical principles into mere rules of thumb.

There is significant slippage between descriptive and normative senses of 'exception' in accounts of emergency. Ferejohn and Pasquino, for instance, have written that "there is a need to recognize exceptional circumstances: wars, invasions, rebellions, and so forth. And given those circumstances, some or all of the operation of constitutional norms might be suspended."[2] Ferejohn and Pasquino contrast exceptions with norms, which they describe *both* as empirical regularities and, following Kelsen as "a command, a prescription, an order."[3] A descriptively exceptional circumstance is one that is out of the ordinary, a statistical outlier or a special situation. But exceptions and emergencies are not co-extensive. Emergencies can continue in effect for long periods of time, as Ferejohn and Pasquino acknowledge.[4] In a case like that of Northern Ireland, emergency was for long stretches the descriptive norm and not the exception, and it would make just as much sense

---

[2] John Ferejohn and Pasquale Pasquino, "The Law of Exception: A Typology of Emergency Powers," p. 220.

[3] Hans Kelsen, *General Theory of Norms*, quoted in Ferejohn and Pasquino, "The Law of Exception," p. 221.

[4] Ferejohn and Pasquino, "The Law of Exception," p. 225.

to ask why violence ceases as to ask, at any given time, why it continues.[5]

Moreover, it does not automatically follow from descriptive exceptionality that norms should be suspended. This would require additional, presumably moral, premises describing the relationship of unusual circumstances to ethical claims. This could take the form of a further principle nullifying or mitigating the principle or right in question, or else of a claim about the hypothetical nature or bounded applicability of moral principles in general. For example, descriptive could slip into normative exception with the addition of the following claim: moral and legal norms are conditioned on a set of circumstances, absent which they cease to have force. Obviously, it would be difficult to accept such a premise without extensive further argument. Such argument is rarely forthcoming in the literature on emergencies, and, as one would expect, still less so in the speeches of statesmen.

Ferejohn and Pasquino seem to offer an implicit moral justification through their functional definition of exceptional circumstances in terms of the powers and rights derogations these circumstances make necessary:

What makes a circumstance exceptional? Sometimes there is a special need for speed or decisional efficiency. Armies need to be created and supplied and moved rapidly from place to place. Some areas of the country might need to be abandoned, and there may be little time to listen to objections from the residents. Or, there may be special needs for secrecy so that opponents will be unable to learn of the nation's aims or plans. Or, there may be a need to stabilize the constitutional system against the nefarious efforts of its enemies. Each of these needs might be met by suspending rights of speech, assembly, and notice that are normally protected constitutionally.[6]

---

[5] Good discussions of the Irish case include Laura Donohue, *Counter-Terrorist Law and Emergency Power in the United Kingdom 1922–2000*; and Robert W. White and Terry Falkenberg White, "Repression and the Liberal State: The Case of Northern Ireland 1969–1972."

[6] Ferejohn and Pasquino, "The Law of Exception," p. 220–1. It is noteworthy that by defining exceptional circumstances in this way, the account would become circular if it was the intention of Ferejohn and Pasquino to provide some kind of justification for derogations. Why can we derogate rights during emergencies? Because the circumstances are exceptional. By definition, exceptional circumstances are those where we can derogate rights. In other words, we can derogate rights because this is one of those situations in which we can derogate rights.

The implication is that 'need' or necessity provides the link, the definitional link, between descriptive and normative exception.

Statesmen often proffer what looks like this same moral middle term: an appeal to necessity. Such appeals can obfuscate more than they clarify. For example, on the occasion of the German invasion of Belgium, Chancellor Theobald von Bethmann Hollweg told the Reichstag, "Gentlemen, we are now in a state of necessity, and necessity knows no law."[7] Germany, called to the aid of its Austro-Hungarian allies, feared that France would be called to the aid of its Russian allies (who, in turn, had been called to the aid of Serbia). Passage through Belgium meant the possibility of immediately knocking out France, and thus avoiding the dangers of a war on two fronts. This was the necessity to which Bethmann Hollweg referred. Implicitly, it served as the middle moral term in his argument before the Reichstag. The circumstances were exceptional, he suggested, and generated a moral necessity to act exceptionally also.

Governor George Torrington declared martial law in Ceylon in 1848. A financial crisis had prompted the already unpopular Governor to impose several new taxes, including a forced labor provision, and a one shilling tax for each pet dog.[8] Riots broke out. The heads of two separate factions declared themselves king. There was sacking and burning. By all accounts this unrest was nonetheless of a fairly minor and containable character. One historian suggests that "contemporary accounts of the 'fighting' might be amusing reading, had not the consequences been so oppressive for the Sinhalese involved in them ..."[9] Torrington unleashed a torrent of military force. While not a single European life had been lost, two hundred Sinhalese were hanged or shot. The burning of houses and public floggings furthered the general terror.[10] Torrington's many local enemies agitated in the United Kingdom sufficiently to bring the matter under investigation by a Parliamentary

---

[7] Reichstag Speech of Chancellor von Bethmann Hollweg, 4 August 1914, on the occasion of the invasion of Belgium. Quoted in Walzer, *Just and Unjust War*, p. 240. The expression *'necessitas non habet legem'* is said to have originated with St. Augustine.

[8] H. A. J. Hulugalle, *British Governors of Ceylon*, p. 77.

[9] E. F. C. Ludowyk, *The Modern History of Ceylon*, p. 79.

[10] Ludowyk, *The Modern History of Ceylon*, p. 80; and Hulugalle, *British Governors of Ceylon*, p. 79.

Committee, on which sat such luminaries as then Prime Minister William Gladstone, as well as former Prime Ministers Sir Robert Peel, and Benjamin Disraeli. In Torrington's defense, Gladstone said: "does not it seem to follow that what he has done has not been done under the law so to be called, but under a necessity which is above the law?"[11]

Both of these men appeal to necessity. But necessity is indeterminate: it has both logical and instrumental varieties. A claim or action can be necessary in itself, or it can follow necessarily from further claims, or else it is necessary for some further aim. Certainly, the Chancellor could not have meant that it was intrinsically necessary for Germany to invade Belgium, that it was logically impossible not to. Nor could Gladstone have intended that Torrington's actions were logically unavoidable. One could hardly say that the actions they describe follow necessarily from some preceding claim, such as a law or a principled commitment. Presumably, Torrington had no principled commitment to the violent suppression of the denizens of Ceylon for its own sake, from which his actions followed. Nor, presumably, did Bethmann Hollweg hold that Germany ought to invade Belgium on principle. Certainly, no law could be found compelling such a course of action.

Implicit in each man's claim was a chain of conditionals. Necessity here is instrumental or 'means-necessity.' It pertains to necessary conditions for the achievement of an end. If Germany did not invade Belgium, then it could not defeat France. If it did not defeat France, it would have to fight a war on two fronts. And if this were the case, then defeat was likely. That defeat in this case would result in general disorder and the destruction of the German state seems less likely, given that, at that very moment, Germany was the aggressor. That is to say, there was another way to avoid defeat: avoid war. Hence, we can see the value of drawing out these conditionals when statesmen make claims of necessity. Implicitly, the Chancellor meant both that German victory was of paramount value and that an iron chain of conditionals led there: invading Belgium was a necessary means to the end of the state's well-being, which was of central importance.[12] Speculation

---

[11] Select Committee on Ceylon, Second Report, 12 Parl. Papers 1850, Question 5477. Quoted in Fairman, *The Law of Martial Rule*, p 48.

[12] Here, he likely confuses power with the preservation of a just order, as statesmen sometimes do. Powerful states sometimes equate a loss of power with total destruction.

about his true ends can be left to the military historians. Similarly, Gladstone perhaps meant to suggest that Torrington's excesses were necessary to bring order and an end to violence. Perhaps he felt this goal preceded law, that order served as a necessary condition for law or justice. These cases are illuminating insofar as they show how necessity stands in as a moral reason for exception while disguising or omitting actual moral content. Means necessity requires ends of significant moral weight.

Gladstone and Bethmann Hollweg suggest, however disingenuously, that the actions in question are morally necessary because they are necessary for the achievement of some trumping moral end. They imply that this end justifies the suspension of other moral and legal rules. The fact that this moral content is rarely made clear by those who appeal to it suggests that claims to moral exceptionalism on the basis of necessity should be met with caution. That there could conceivably be some moral content in means-necessity claims is apparent. But no moral explanation for what could count as a trumping moral end is yet forthcoming. Hence, we still lack a justification for slipping from descriptive into normative exceptionalism.

And there are further problems. Even if a statesman established the existence of a trumping moral end that gave content to necessity, and even if he then proffered a cogent chain of conditionals for achieving it, this would still be insufficient to justify the suspension of the moral rule. Indeed, there are good reasons to oppose such a course of action. For legal and moral norms, as opposed to statistical or sociocultural norms, cannot admit exceptions and remain normative. A simple exception to a moral rule would call the nature of the rule itself into question. If moral norms cease to apply in hard cases, what gives them moral force? How are they different from other kinds of maxims?[13] The notion of blame would cease to make sense. One could no longer claim that they ever are, whether substantively, as in the case of deontological moral rules, or procedurally, as in the case of consequentialist rules, imperatives. Exception drains the meaning of ethics and their force.

---

[13] Interesting discussions of the role of maxims in political ethics can be found in Ray Nichols, "Maxims, 'Practical Wisdom,' and the Language of Action: Beyond Grand Theory"; and in ethics more generally in D. S. Shwayder, "Moral Maxims and Moral Rules."

Hence, whatever means we come to for understanding the ethics of emergency, we must avoid making exceptions by suspending moral rules and we must give moral content to the idea of necessity. The balance of this chapter presents such a means, based on an ethical-political pluralism. This pluralism is a constant feature of political life and the conflicts that arise inside this constant plurality of ethical-political principles can be mediated through *action* rather than through deliberation aimed at promoting abstract consistency. Relying on an ethics of experience, this framework fulfills both conditions while maintaining the possibility of both emergency action and accountability.

ETHICAL-POLITICAL PLURALISM

All moral life is infused with conflict, a multiplicity of values that are not necessarily consistent. Emergency action, when it is justified at all, is justifiable on the basis of a further value: the preservation of the state order. Order is one aspect of what I called, in Chapter 2, existential ethics. I want now to revive this terminology in a liberal, rather than a republican context. Recall that I defined existential ethics as those related to the creation or preservation of a state in contrast with quotidian ethics that govern the day to day activity of a state. In the work of republican exceptionalists, the glory of a republican form of government served as an implicit justification for a two-tier exceptionalist ethics that eclipsed quotidian ethics. Liberal values will here take their place, but with the proviso that they will not be eclipsed. In the case of a liberal democracy, liberal values constitute quotidian ethics animating the day-to-day functions of a political order, while existential ethics invoke different principles for the preservation of the liberal democratic order. For example, civil and human rights, due process, distributive justice, and ethnic and gender equality are all aspects of liberal quotidian ethics. Liberal democracies under emergency powers can remain liberal by not allowing existential ethics to suspend the moral weight of quotidian liberal ethics. Here is how.

In a liberal democracy, moral ends serve as reasons why derogating civil rights and ethical-political values sometimes seems necessary. Although these moral ends may not be strictly liberal in character, the scope of liberalism need not be co-extensive with the scope of political ethics in liberal democracies more generally. It becomes possible to see how this could be so if, as Chapter 3 showed we ought to, we put aside the neo-Kantian focus on abstract consistency. Extra-liberal values and conflicts between and among them are pervasive in the moral life of liberal democracies, and order has a peculiar status among them.

Security, order, desert, group cohesion, cultural pluralism, and the preservation and expression of cultural heritage are not liberal values. They are only peripherally connected with liberty or with political equality. Nonetheless, they are widely apparent and widely valued in the policies and state sponsored pursuits of liberal democratic societies. Few would advocate the allocation of political office, of jobs, or even of university places through the most egalitarian means: drawing lots.[14] Allocation on the basis of merit has at least an equal weight. Furthermore, the value of culture and collective history is apparent in the special rights of indigenous peoples protected in the constitutions of liberal democratic states such as Canada and New Zealand.[15] And many liberal democracies, including the United States, Canada, and the member states of the European Union, spend funds on the promotion and protection of cultural heritage, through designated historic sites and sometimes through restrictions on foreign cultural content. The Constitution of Switzerland (2001) goes so far as to guarantee, in Article 88, the maintenance and preservation of hiking and footpaths.

It has been a fashion in the liberal thought of the last two decades to attempt to show how these apparently illiberal values might actually be derived from liberalism.[16] The intellectual acrobatics these texts display tend to result in antinomies, such as Kymlicka's paradox of internal minorities: by following Joseph Raz in grounding the value of culture in the value of choice, Kymlicka is hard pressed to explain

---

[14] A recent exception may be found in John McCormick, "Contain the Wealthy and Patrol the Magistrates: Restoring Elite Accountability to Popular Government."

[15] Canada, *Constitution Act* (1982), Article 35. *The Treaty of Waitangi* (1840) considered a part of New Zealand's constitution, accords special rights to the Maori and guarantees protection of their interests. Because of the differences in the English and Maori texts of the documents, which in some cases are radical, legal decisions often refer simply to the 'principles' of the Treaty. See http://www.treatyofwaitangi. govt.nz, accessed 22 December 2004.

[16] See, for instance, Yael Tamir, *Liberal Nationalism*; Will Kymlicka, *Liberalism, Community, and Culture*; Will Kymlicka, *Multicultural Citizenship*; and Joseph Raz, *The Morality of Freedom*.

the paradox of cultures that restrict choice or accord it on the basis of sexist or racist criteria.[17] Values like multiculturalism may well be connected with liberal values at various points, but, unless liberalism is contorted in fantastic ways, they are not themselves liberal values. 'Merit' and 'culture' are only peripherally connected with equal liberty.

One might suggest that, if these values are inconsistent with liberal values, they will either constitute an insurmountable objection to liberalism, or else one must concede that they are not values after all. If they can't go together, by *reductio ad absurdum*, one of them will have to go. But this is only a problem if abstract consistency is cast as an ultimate value in the first place, a view that is arguably *itself* incoherent.[18]

Conflicts between values are a constant feature of the ethical-political landscape, even with respect to rights derogations, which are certainly not special to emergencies. Rights come into conflict with other rights or with other values all the time. One need not look far for evidence: in the International Covenant on Civil and Political Rights (ICCPR), as well as the Covenant on Economic, Social, and Cultural Rights, nearly every article contains explicit principles governing its limitation. The ICCPR contains a variety of different kinds of limitations, such as Article 4 (1), which explicitly allows for derogations in times of emergency, Article 8 (3a), which allows for "slave" labor of those detained on criminal charges, and in Article 6 (1) and Article 9 (1) people can be deprived of their right to life or liberty, so long as this is not done arbitrarily. In fact, nearly every right comes along with built-in limitations.

These find clear echoes in most domestic constitutional rights regimes. For example, freedom of thought, conscience, and religion is guaranteed in the ICCPR, in Article 18, as well as in the Constitutions of most liberal democracies. Yet this freedom is sometimes restricted when it clearly conflicts with other rights and values. A religion that calls for an active program of conversion may run into conflict with the very right to free conscience that protects it. A religion that calls for

---

[17] See Lazar, "The Scope of Liberalism: Implications of the Ethico-Political Status of Ethnic Minorities for the Relationship of Liberal Theory to Political Morality"; and also, Leslie Green, "Internal Minorities and their Rights."

[18] Isaiah Berlin has argued along these lines in "The Pursuit of the Ideal," pp. 1–19.

bigamy, or for any kind of violence may face legal restrictions in a liberal democratic society as well. In general, in accordance with John Locke's ideas about toleration, religious practice is free (or, for Locke, tolerated) up until the point where it requires its adherents to break the law. At that point, exceptions are sometimes made, and this seems to vary with the seriousness of the legal breach. So, for example, exceptions to drug laws are sometimes made to allow for the practice of indigenous religions. Exceptions to laws about public schooling have been made in the service of religious freedom, as in the ruling in the famous case *Wisconsin v. Yoder*. In this case, the United States Supreme Court found that the requirement of the law that children must attend school until the age of sixteen violated the religious freedom of Amish children, whose parents believed that high school education endangered their children's salvation. Yet even in this decision – indeed in most decisions of constitutional courts – the importance of competing values is keenly apparent. The decision makes reference to evidence that the Amish provide an adequate vocational education to their children, outside school, and, in a dissenting opinion on education and the childrens' right to opportunity, Justice William O. Douglas wrote that a child

may want to be a pianist or an astronaut or an oceanographer . . . It is the student's judgment, not his parents', that is essential if we are to give full meaning to what we have said about the Bill of Rights and of the right of students to be masters of their own destiny. If . . . his education is truncated, his entire life may be stunted and deformed. The child, therefore, should be given an opportunity to be heard before the State gives the exemption which we honor today.[19]

The right to freedom of religion is not absolute, but may potentially be derogated when other interests of critical importance are taken into account. The same may be said for freedom of expression, where we habitually make restrictions on the basis of other values: no matter how free our speech, it is never so free that we can shout 'Fire!' in a theater, thereby endangering the lives of patrons. Free speech is important, but so is the safeguarding of life. And this exception is not only esoteric. In many jurisdictions, hate speech is disallowed, fomenting rebellion or encouraging violence is sometimes restricted, and one cannot spread

[19] *Wisconsin v. Yoder*, 406 U.S. 205 (1972).

damaging lies about a person in a public forum. The interest that we have in free expression is not absolute either. This raises questions about our habit of thinking of rights as trumps. They may provide a strong hand, but not necessarily a trumping one.

Why shouldn't liberal and other values conflict, when, after all, values within liberalism often conflict? Where liberal values conflict, neither value is necessarily lexically prior, but nor are they entirely consistent. That values of culture, order, efficiency, and merit might sometimes conflict is no more a matter for concern than the fact that liberal values like freedom and equality sometimes conflict.

This is no surprise, considering that the world is irreducibly complex. However unlikely the prospect of its complete physical description, its moral description is yet less likely. It would be remarkable if our concepts and ideas in general mapped neatly and consistently onto the world. Indeed, even if our concepts, ideas, and principles were simply a mirror reflection of 'the way things are,' it could only follow that these concepts, ideas, and principles could be consistent *if the phenomena themselves were consistent.* When these are human phenomena, as in the case of ethics, this seems unlikely. Indeed, it would be particularly surprising if an ethical-political doctrine like liberalism just so happened to be coextensive with political ethics, because liberal values have grown out of particular times and circumstances, in response to particular political problems. When new problems, or new manifestations of old problems, arise, highly abstract principles and values will have different manifestations and modes of application.

This recognition of conflict among rights and between rights and other values is not relativism but a descriptive kind of pluralism. To be open to such a pluralism and to embrace conflicting principles provides a clearer reflection of moral life. What is lost in terms of the aesthetics of completeness is gained by enriching accuracy and subtlety.

A liberalism of experience, in contrast with a rational-deductive liberalism, allows for conflict and praises accuracy over abstract consistency. Recognizing the mix of values that animate liberal democratic societies, in addition to being more faithful to the phenomena, actually strengthens liberalism, since it shows that the importance of external values does not negate the importance of liberal values. On this view, it is no critique of liberalism to show that community or patriotism also matter. The value of multiculturalism, on such a view, does not negate the value of individual autonomy, it joins it. Nor is it a critique of liberal values to show, as Carl Schmitt and his contemporary followers hope to, that liberalism excludes decisiveness and order.

Indeed, among those values external to liberalism, order takes a central position. It serves as a countervailing value that animates emergency powers in liberal democracies. The preservation of order, the maintenance of the state in a functional form, is what justifies what looks like making an exception (when it *is* justified). It is what emergency action is necessary *for*, the animating force of existential ethics.

The restoration of order through emergency action in liberal democracies is governed by a system of ethics, rather than by a state of exception from ethics. This follows from the claims, to be established here, that the order embodied in the liberal democratic state has moral worth, and that there is a second order obligation to preserve things of moral worth.

We can conceive of order in the abstract, absent any content, as a system of rules and a means of enforcement. But in practice, any actual order (as opposed to an abstract concept of order) has moral content, and hence is just or unjust to varying degrees. So to say that an order has moral worth is thus not to say that order has value in itself. This would be a contentless statement because there is no such thing as a contentless order. Order consists of rules and means of enforcement. But rules have origins and context, and rules embody principles and pursue further aims, all of these just or unjust. Rules are instituted autocratically or not, are egalitarian or not. Order always has effects beyond everything in its place because we can always question the placement itself. Hence, order takes on the moral character of the origins, content, and effects of the rules of which it consists and only those orders that embody morally worthy principles are themselves of moral worth.

I have taken as an assumption that the values and principles embodied (if not always effectively fulfilled) by liberal democratic states are ones we hold desirable. Many of these core values are related to rights and their enforcement. The moral worth of the liberal democratic state stems from its embodiment of liberal democratic values and its capacity to ensure predictability and security according to standards of justice embodied in, for example, civil and human rights. The organization and enforcement capacity of this mode of order also enables the pursuit of worthy ends such as those described in the positive rights of some of the United Nations covenants and declarations. All of this enables the individual and collective pursuit of arts, sciences, commerce, and the protection and development of culture, environment, heritage, and so on.

The idea that a state order has intrinsic value may conjure ghosts of fascism or of the worst kinds of nationalism. This kind of worry, and an accompanying metaphysics, is reflected in Nozick's statement that "there is no *social entity* with a good that undergoes some sacrifice for its own good. There are only individual people."[20] I will not add here to the mass of argument that has accumulated against this and similar claims. It will suffice to point out that this is not the common subjective experience. Most citizens of liberal democratic states feel some kind of affection for their country, in no small part because of the values it embodies and represents, but also because of a sense of connection to history and culture (or histories and cultures). Citizens reify and grow attached to a state that serves as an instrument enabling collective endeavor and embodying collective values. To the extent that a state develops collective symbols, a collective history, institutions, and so on, it becomes easier to personify and it takes on value of its own. Both introspection and the existence of voluntary armies in wartime attest to this process.[21]

A state's intrinsic value stems from constant conjunction: it is infused with the values through which it is constituted and that it pursues and protects. Nozick is wrong about social entities. To the extent that a state order pursues and protects liberal values such as a commitment to rights, or to freedom, equality, and human flourishing somehow conceived, accepting its intrinsic moral worth need not be sinister.

That the order-enforcing function of many states is also instrumentally valuable is broadly acknowledged, articulated most carefully by contract theorists such as Rousseau, Kant, and Hobbes. Morally and socially worthy aims can be achieved when there is security in the

---

[20] Robert Nozick, *Anarchy, State, and Utopia*, p. 33.
[21] An interesting account of this understudied matter of voluntary armies is found in Steven Smith, "Hegel's Views on War, the State, and International Relations."

predictable respect for rights. Rousseau's state enables justice, duty, and right.[22] For Hobbes, famously, the well-ordered state enables not only justice but *everything* of value:

> In [a disordered] condition, there is no place for Industry; because the fruit thereof is uncertain: and consequently no Culture of the Earth; no Navigation, nor use of the commodities that may be imported by Sea; no commodious Building; Instruments of moving, and removing such things as require much force; no Knowledge of the face of the Earth; no account of Time; no Arts; no Letters; no Society.[23]

Security provides the soil in which autonomy flourishes also. Fear is not conducive to cultivation or actualization, both because self-protection takes effort and concentration and because planning is difficult in an atmosphere of extreme uncertainty.

But beyond the benefits of physical security, the state has the capacity to coordinate, which allows for the aggressive collective pursuit of moral ends connected with basic needs and basic rights. At a minimum, the capacity to coordinate can ensure we all drive on the same side of the road. Through providing security and coordination, the state is instrumentally valuable for the achievement of moral ends.

This instrumental kind of value is partly constituted through enforcement. Force is a large part of a state's ordering function, and one source of our queasiness about it. Yet, we cannot do without this ordering force, if, pragmatically perhaps, we take humans as they are and not as they might be. Order always requires a mechanism of enforcement. At one extreme there is Rawls's 'fact of oppression':

> [It is a] general fact . . . that a continued shared understanding on one comprehensive religious, philosophical, or moral doctrine can be maintained only by the oppressive use of state power . . . . [Even] a society united on a reasonable form of utilitarianism, or on the reasonable liberalisms of Kant or Mill, would likewise

---

[22] Jean-Jacques Rousseau, *Du contrat social*, I.8.

[23] Thomas Hobbes, *Leviathan*, ch. 13. It is interesting to note the complete reversal that Joseph de Maistre later effects, arguing that all that is great, all those things that Hobbes here cites, grow from the bloodsoaked soil of the battlefield. Chaos, and not order, yields the fruits of genius.

require the sanctions of state power to remain so. Call this 'the fact of oppression.'[24]

This holds true even if oppression is inconsistent with the liberalisms of Kant or Mill. Reason is only reasonable with those who wish to reason too, and it is an empirical fact, at least taking men as they are, not as they might be, that not everyone, not every group, shares this wish. No matter how reasonable an order, which is to say no matter how much it may command universal assent in the abstract, there will always be those within and without who reject and fight against it. At the other extreme there is simple banditry. If we accept a Rousseauan style perfectibility thesis – that under perfect institutions humans may come to be perfect – then *eventually* force would be redundant, but it would still be required in the medium term. If not, we must accept that order will always require enforcement.

Force is a tense but essential part of order, and order, we have seen, is intrinsically and instrumentally valuable. Order's value can be intrinsic because it embodies predictability and the reification of broader values. Its value can be instrumental through the good things predictability enables and for the moral aims coordination enables. It follows from this that not all states are intrinsically and instrumentally valuable nor can force in the service of preserving order always be justified. Emergency powers and the existential ethics that underlie them are not justified in every case. Arguably, insurrection or invasion is sometimes perfectly justified. In such cases existential ethics have no force. Only justly ordered states can act on the basis of existential ethics, and hence only some kinds of states could justly make use of emergency powers. An apartheid state is not worth preserving because the values that characterize it and that it embodies and enforces are not worth preserving. There would be no moral justification, at least along the lines presented here, for emergency powers in an apartheid state.

This demonstrates further why Carl Schmitt's exceptionalism in particular is unsatisfactory. Schmitt's decisionism implicitly aims to

---

[24] In this passage, Rawls is not suggesting that oppression is therefore always a necessity, since he believes his overlapping consensus perspective overcomes this problem. However, insofar as one defensible perspective is that there must be only one perspective, pluralism, although less substantive than Kantian liberalism, fares no better. See John Rawls, *Political Liberalism*, p. 37.

preserve order as such, and Schmitt claims this ordering is executed in the absence of norms. But the decisions a decisionist sovereign makes cannot help but have a moral character since the order defended has a moral character. Maintaining the status quo is also a moral choice. Unless there can be rules and structures that are amoral, there can be nothing that is *order as such*, that is worthy in itself. Hence, Schmitt must smuggle normative criteria in through the back door.[25]

Now, it is evident from the absurdity of the alternative that there is an obligation to protect, with the least odious means, an order that embodies morally worthy principles. For, if we are under an obligation, by necessary implication we are under a further obligation to find means of meeting it. We are obliged to 'bring it about.' There are generally multiple means to achieving an end and hence the second order obligation to employ means to a worthy end takes the form of a disjunctive proposition. An obligation to be charitable implies an obligation to acquire the means of charity: either to set aside time or to set aside money. It matters from where such time or money is diverted: missing a television program or a day of work, or missing time spent with or even feeding one's children. Alternatively, one could rob a bank. But a duty to act charitably with no corresponding duty to find means to charitability is absurd.

The disjunctive shows how this argument is not a blanket Machiavellian claim that the end justifies the means. It demonstrates that the least morally odious means are the only *potentially* justified means. Our second order obligation is to preserve and employ the most moral means to meet moral obligations. We might call this 'the most moral means principle,' and this principle marks the end of the first part of the argument for the moral possibility of rights derogations.

The argument thus far has taken the following form. Liberal values are not co-extensive with political values, even in a liberal democracy. Recognizing other values does not negate liberal values, even when they conflict. Instead, a liberal democratic state, and probably any state, embodies a robust plurality of values. One of these is order, the end of existential ethics and the end of emergency powers. Order in turn makes possible the effective preservation of life, and the protection of

[25] Leo Strauss makes a related argument in his "Notes on Carl Schmitt, the Concept of the Political," reprinted in Carl Schmitt, *The Concept of the Political*, p. 101.

rights and other liberal values. An order's intrinsic worth is constituted by the other values it embodies or protects, and hence only those orders that embody and protect just values are justified in employing emergency powers or exercising existential ethics. The instrumental and intrinsic value of a liberal democratic order thus stems from its protection and promotion of liberal rights and of other good things.

It follows from all of this that order and justice are not strictly separable. There is an intrinsic connection between liberal democratic order as an entity and the rights whose protection or derogation is a matter for present concern. This order itself is made actual, is given content, by exactly those rights that constitute one part of justice. The two may appear to be opposed, to require weighing and balancing, but their relationship is more complicated. Without rights, liberal democratic order would be contentless, and without order to describe rules and their enforcement, rights would be potential only. Even the capacity to exercise rights grows out of membership in a community.

However one conceives of rights, the state is necessary to their fruition, either through their creation, their actualization, or, minimally but critically, through their enforcement. The fact of their description is not sufficient to bring rights into the world, but rather to bring them into a state of potentiality. Rights must be formalized to have weight and enforceability.[26] Rights help delineate the bounds and content of just order and a just order makes rights actual through delineation and enforcement. Whether or not humans are born equal in dignity and moral rights, without the civic rights of a citizen their abstract equality does them little good.

That the capacity to exercise rights is bound up with membership in a well-functioning political community is among Hannah Arendt's claims in *The Origins of Totalitarianism*. Arendt argues that the fundamental right is the 'right to have rights' by which she means the right to membership in a state.[27] Burke's concrete rights as an Englishman, Arendt concurred, were of more use to him than the Frenchman's abstract rights as a man. To have rights requires more than that one be recognized as a human animal. It requires that one be treated as a

---

[26] For an interesting discussion of this topic, see Stephen Holmes and Cass Sunstein, *The Cost of Rights*.

[27] Hannah Arendt, *The Origins of Totalitarianism*, p. 296ff.

creature with agency. Arendt implies that membership in an organized community is prerequisite to effectual thought or action. There is no meaningful action outside of an organized community, and hence membership in such a community is a necessary condition for rights.

Citizenship in a state and the liberal democratic character of that state are necessary to the actualization or at least to the enforcement of rights in addition to the catalogue of broader benefits. The moral character of the state, in turn, is constituted by these rights. Order and justice, in this case, are inextricable.

We can now see how an existential ethics and the order it protects are a justified aspect of the pluralism I am advocating. The state plays no small part in enforcing and enabling political ethics. Through its constitution and solemnification of rights in official documents, through public education and public display to make those rights treasured and respected, through the creation of a community in which agency is possible, and through the financing of its courts for rights' protection, the liberal democratic state order constitutes itself by means of these constitutionally identified rights and they stand at its core as its essence. To the extent that a liberal democratic order constitutes a just order, it is justifiable to work for its preservation.[28] Hence, emergency powers themselves take on a moral character when employed within acceptable bounds to preserve a state of sufficient moral worth.

THE SCOPE OF EXISTENTIAL ETHICS

Now, if order and liberal rights entail one another, it follows that existential ethics are a constant and not exceptional feature of liberal democratic life. What I have called existential ethics obviously manifest as emergency powers in times of crisis. But the enforcement and preservation of order, however more urgent in times of emergency, is a central

---

[28] I leave open the question of whether other forms of political order could justify emergency powers. Emergencies constitute a special problem for liberal democracies, insofar as they involve the concentration of power and the derogation of rights. The prevention of domination by means of separated powers and civil rights is a hallmark of liberal democracy. However, to the extent this was a problem in some other regime type, the question of emergency powers' defensibility presumably would always be correlated with the moral defensibility of the regime.

function of everyday government and one that *always* involves the derogation of rights. If this is true, then emergency powers need no special justification at all. Instead, they are an extension of everyday practice and everyday values. The difference is of degree and not of kind.

The clearest example of how existential ethics functions in everyday political life is the enforcement of the criminal law. For, in addition to those emergency threats to order that are sudden and overwhelming states must contend with crime, which threatens order gradually but no less seriously. The state would not disintegrate if some crime went unpunished. But we have established that enforcement is a necessary element of order. In everyday political life, order is enforced through the threat of punishment or the actualization of punishment, which, stripped of the values that context overlays, involves violating the fundamental human and civil rights of the person punished. Even in those jurisdictions that respect human rights to the extent that capital or other corporal punishment is outlawed, locking people in cells could hardly, in any other context, be viewed as other than a gross abuse of rights. Some might object that to take law enforcement out of context, to call punishment a rights violation, removes the very salient (though very illiberal) element of desert. In addition to order, desert is certainly a value that animates punishment on nearly every account, except a simple utilitarian one. But it is only for a pure retributivist that desert constitutes the sole justification for punishment. The pure retributivist's claim would be that order and public safety are irrelevant. Those whom we punish deserve harm and have forfeited their rights. *Fiat justitia pereat mundi.* In breaking the law, people knowingly makes themselves subject to such treatment. While this is true, it seems to tidily equate the administration of justice with what, absent the context, is clearly a literal derogation of rights. By denying that this 'counts' as a rights violation, we imply that the rules, which is to say certain rights, are no longer in effect for those who violate the law. If we take this perspective, retributivism, which forms part of nearly every theory of punishment, would then become the moral counterpart of exceptionalism. Although most would allow that punishment serves a broader social function, deterring citizens and other denizens from committing crimes, part of this deterrence is dependent on an awareness of desert and its function. Furthermore, some element of desert is implicit in the very concept of punishment: one cannot punish the innocent except metaphorically or by mistake. So this is a serious matter. It seems that some rights, for us, are either contingent on good, law-abiding behavior or are derogable on occasion when, with due seriousness, we consider competing values. In liberal democracies, serious rights derogations for the sake of order are not just for special occasions.

The parallels between crime and emergencies and between law enforcement and emergency powers are many, but there are, of course, important differences. Genuine emergencies threaten the infrastructure necessary to furthering rights and collective values, or urgently threaten the rights or physical well-being of citizens on a grand scale. Criminal activity threatens the same, but on a smaller or more gradual scale. Emergencies present a serious and imminent threat to life and property in a given area. A serious earthquake theatens everyone's physical integrity and property, infrastructure which everyone uses and without which the state is dysfunctional, is threatened or destroyed and all of this happens at once. A war threatens every citizen and the integrity of the nation itself, and, again, its effects are not gradual. Munitions are needed *now*. A spy ring or sabotage plot must be foiled *now*. Facing an emergency may simply require so much human power that the police cannot manage on their own. *Urgency* and *scale* differentiate emergency threats to order from more quotidian cases.[29]

Questions of urgency and scale mean that, during emergencies, due process protections are sometimes curtailed. Rules of evidence for apprehending and holding suspects are relaxed, and preventive detention without charge, or, in the case of the United States, even the suspension of habeas corpus, is rendered more or less legal.[30] It is these emergency rights derogations that concern us most, as they leave individuals most vulnerable to state abuse. It is true that it is often to access

---

[29] Of course, there is a range of urgency and a range of scale. A localized epidemic is urgent but it may not reach the scale of a threatened nuclear attack. Scaled legislation, such as Canada's *Emergencies Act* (1985), takes account of this. Nonetheless, Kim Lane Scheppele has suggested, with merit, that recognizing a wider scale can actually be detrimental. In "Small Emergencies" (pp. 835–6) she argues that "The very idea that emergencies could be minor . . . suggests that they are not to be seen as fundamentally disruptive of the overall order of things, or of the prospects for realization of a constitutional ideal."

[30] I do not mean to suggest that all of these are necessarily justifiable. The suspension of habeas corpus in particular is difficult to justify, and certainly runs contrary to international guidelines on emergency powers.

exactly these powers of derogation that states of emergency are declared. In other words, one might object that exactly those safeguards that protect citizens subject to the criminal justice system are those suspended during emergencies.[31]

Where a fundamental principle is violated, however, there may be more than one means to an end. Here we can only look to the principles expressed through rights talk to guide creative institutional design, and this is nothing new because such conflicts reflect a difference in degree and not kind. Resource scarcity means that due process is only roughly enforced in the normal criminal justice system as well. Legal aid clients do not receive the same level of service as the clients of prominent private lawyers because this would be prohibitively expensive. Police officers fail to follow up on every call and cut corners when facing heavy caseloads. Everyday criminal procedures in most common law systems allow for individuals to be locked up on remand, or held without bail, sometimes for months – again because of scarce resources and strong suspicion – prior to a trial and conviction.

This is no different in kind from detention of espionage, treason, or terror suspects during an emergency, so long as the process of their detention is set out clearly in advance and so long as there are time limitations, means of recourse, and after the fact compensation for any wrongful imprisonment. Hence, emergency detention does not strictly go beyond the de facto mandate of the everyday criminal law. Restrictions on due process protections reflect a relative resource scarcity. This is the same unfortunate reason why those subject to the criminal justice system under normal circumstances often have their due process protections curtailed. I do not mean to suggest that this is acceptable and it is certainly undesirable. I mean only to suggest that the two kinds of rights derogation are closely related. In extensions of rights derogations that are based on resource scarcity, there is continuity for the ultimate sake of order. These tragic cases are not the exceptional purview of emergencies.

---

[31] On this, see Stephanos Stavros, "The Right to a Fair Trial in Emergency Situations." Stavros compares the provisions in the various international human rights organs and concludes that while "A minimum floor of fair trial does appear to exist in emergency situations," enforcement mechanisms are shaky (p. 364).

Of course urgency and scale make emergency powers descriptively different. The rules are altered, special powers are made available. If the matter were manageable through normal means, states would be required to so manage them.[32] When the state order through which norms and laws are normally enforced is threatened, the order itself is threatened.[33] What makes the declaration necessary is the incapacity of the police to manage scale and urgency because of resource restrictions and lack of time. Urgency and scale differentiate normalcy and emergency but they are differences of degree and not of kind. Existential ethics function constantly, but what they entail or justify will shift if the matter at hand is urgent and far-reaching.

Rights derogations and resource-based restrictions on due process protections are tragic when they occur in the day-to-day criminal justice system, just as rights derogations under emergency powers are tragic. Because order and justice entail each other, an existential ethics does not overrule a quotidian liberal ethics in the criminal justice system any more than it does under emergency powers. But both are an integral part of liberal democratic order and both would benefit from a clearer articulation of principles. This would minimize the scope for abuse, and would necessitate suitable gravity in confronting the moral violations they involve. We should be nonchalant about neither. We should aim to minimize both.

Hence, there is no reason to sharply separate the normal functioning of government from the functioning of government under emergency circumstances. We need not court the dangers of the norm/exception dichotomy. If I am right that criminal law and emergency powers can be justified (when they are justifiable) on the same grounds, and that the differences between them are of degree and not kind, then there is no reason to think of emergency powers as normatively or descriptively exceptional. The protection of order is a normal, and not exceptional

---

[32] For a complete account of what international standards mandate, see Robert Lillich, "The Paris Minimum Standards of Human Rights Norms in a State of Emergency."

[33] Section 371 of the Constitution of South Africa (1996) states: "A state of emergency may be declared ... only *when the life of the nation is threatened* ... and the declaration is necessary to restore peace and order" (my italics). This phrasing is interesting, because of the ambiguity of the word 'life.' The life of the nation could refer to its continuing bare existence. Alternatively, it could indicate a condition of vibrancy and vivacity, the buzz of the nation: in other words, its proper functioning. This shows one possible advantage of scaled legislation.

part of statecraft. It demonstrates a value pluralism that, while implicit in liberal democracy, is rarely drawn out by normative theorists.

PRACTICAL CONSISTENCY

The plurality of values that shows how emergency powers might be justified – when they *are* in fact justified – is messy and inconsistent. For, acting according to a countervailing moral principle like 'preserve just orders' does not mean exculpation from the imperative of respecting rights. Even intrinsically connected values can be incommensurable, and the same action can and should be judged simultaneously according to these different moral criteria. Were theoretical consistency our primary concern, the argument would face a major difficulty. But one benefit of the approach to political ethics taken here is that abstract consistency becomes a less central feature. The function of ethics as a guide to right action comes to the fore. To the extent that a consistent *action* is necessary, it is worth exploring how consistency might be rendered in practice, instead of in theory.

To resolve a moral conflict at the level of theory would mean providing an overarching rule with substantive or procedural elements. A consequentialist , for instance, could easily mediate the conflict by means of the overarching rule 'maximize utility.'[34] A neo-Kantian might offer a different kind of overarching rule, such as John Rawls's procedural principle of lexical ordering.[35] For example: "order and basic security must be established and maintained. The state must be preserved. Once order is established through the state, justice and rights must be upheld and enforced." Neither of these kinds of principles could do the job.

The utilitarian principle yields the unsatisfactory result that certain morally serious considerations cease to matter once the equation has been computed.[36] Such a perspective is advanced by, for instance,

---

[34] John Stuart Mill, for instance, advocates utilitarianism as a means of deciding between conflicting principles of justice. See *Utilitarianism*, p. 54.

[35] John Rawls, *Theory of Justice*, p. 38. Posner and Vermeule, in their article "Emergencies and Democratic Failure" (p. 1098), also reject the possibility of lexical ordering of rights to security and freedom.

[36] This is clear if we consider the accounts of moral-military dilemmas of some famous utilitarians. See R. M. Hare, "Rules of War and Moral Reasoning," and R. B. Brandt, "Utilitarianism and the Rules of War."

Richard Posner. Posner holds that the kind of pure legal Kantianism espoused by the German Constitutional Court in their decision on the *Aviation Security Act* is naïve. For Posner, rights, constitutions, laws, and so on are all tools of convenience that can and should be changed or circumvented where appropriate for reaching 'optimal' ends. Even torture can be morally – even if not legally – justified.[37] To see why such a perspective is morally wanting, consider the example of Winston Churchill and the bombing of Coventry. If we imagine, in November of 1940, Winston Churchill has intelligence from the 'Enigma' machine suggesting that Coventry is to be bombed, then he has an obligation to protect the lives of the people of that city by warning them. He also has an obligation to win the war. This will be more difficult were the flow of intelligence from Enigma to stop. The utilitarian decides by comparing the potential suffering of the people of Coventry with the effects on all if World War II is prolonged or lost through the cessation of easy intelligence.[38] But a utilitarian overarching rule, insofar as it effectively cancels some obligations, does not provide for guilt or regret. It implies that, once the calculation has been executed, the right course is clear and also morally clear. Coventry and its denizens no longer have relevance, on this view. But it would be a sort of willful (if understandable) blindness not to recognize that the loss of the citizens of Coventry means something beyond the outcome of the equation. Accuracy and nuance must be matters for concern when stakes are so high. It is better to avoid reductionism where feasible.

The neo-Kantian principle, by contrast, allows for the preservation of moral significance because no element ceases to matter. But, here, too, there are insurmountable problems. How can one lexically order principles of order and justice (or of existential and quotidian ethics) when the two principles are inseparable? Order cannot be secured prior to rights because liberal democratic order and its value are largely constituted by these rights and their enforcement. At the same time, it is incoherent to insist on the preservation of rights at any cost, because they are embodied in the state's order, which is also necessary

---

[37] Richard Posner, *Not a Suicide Pact.*
[38] For a good account of the Enigma adventure, see F. H. Hinsley, *British Intelligence in the Second World War*, pp. 47–8.

to their preservation and enforcement. Justice and order are inextricably linked, and hence can have no lexical order.

Arguably, any overarching principle, whether deontological or consequentialist would face similar problems. But there is no reason to decide definitely and at the level of theory how existential and quotidian ethics should be mediated in any given instance. Once a variety of principles are carefully specified, they can enter practical deliberation in the same manner that a single moral principle would.

The role of concrete moral deliberation and judgment in ethics is not widely acknowledged outside of neo-Aristotelian thought.[39] Yet, it constitutes an important alternative to forcing moral notions into abstract consistency, against the grain. Instead of simply choosing the right rule and how to apply it, we choose the right action (or try to), taking into account a number of rules. Consistency comes at the level of practice, not in the abstract.

This is the way in which we sometimes come to difficult decisions on courses of action in more general terms. Many factors and principles enter into settling on a course of action. Some of these are moral, while others are practical and concern such things as efficiency, preferences, and so on. A diversity of moral considerations could easily figure in a manner broadly similar to that of nonmoral preferences with the caveat that regret and even shame must accompany a violation of *any* moral principle, even in favor of a further moral principle. Moral reasons unlike other kinds of reasons are obligatory. But this means only that, in failing to act accordingly, one is culpable. We do not demand consistency of reasons more generally and we need not with moral reasons either. But, when moral reasons conflict, culpability remains for the course not taken. Regret and shame are appropriate. In this way, consistency comes through our *actions*.

Practical wisdom involves deliberation. Deliberation implies a condition in which there is significant uncertainty (for, how could we deliberate about what is certain?), but where sufficient grounds and means of justification exist to establish a basis for claims. The concept

---

[39] Charles Larmore has advocated the revival of an Aristotelian, judgment-centered perspective in dealing with moral complexity. See his *Patterns of Moral Complexity*. See also Ronald Beiner, *Political Judgment*; Elijah Millgram (ed.), *Varieties of Practical Reasoning*.

of deliberation in the democratic context, for example with respect to choosing policies, is so commonplace that practical wisdom and judgment with respect to ethical action, a rendering consistent in practice, should not seem strange. We should no sooner expect abstract consistency from political ethics than from policy making.

Allowing the moral theory of emergency powers to reflect the moral nuances and complexity of states of emergency might allow or even require multiple moral evaluations and hence multiple moral judgments. This should not be surprising. All social description is irreducibly complex.[40] Why should moral description be any different, so long as it does not preclude action or judgment? And it need do so no more than a multiplicity of nonmoral reasons precludes action. Beyond procedural constraints, clarified moral principles, and the absolute bounds set by international law, a political leader need not have a ready rule that tells her what to do in advance nor do citizens need to have such a rule in order to judge. In fact, we would be hard pressed to think of any political circumstance in which it was otherwise.

A statesman can arrive at a course of action and citizens can judge it through deliberation that takes the weight of all moral elements seriously and mediates them through the practical wisdom that comes of an experience of virtuous living. Real complexity can be coherently maintained and relevant agency is not precluded, nor is judgment robbed of its teeth.

This emphasis on deliberation may seem at odds with the function of emergency powers. One reason that the concentration of powers is an important part of emergency powers is that speed is often of the essence. Fewer parties means speedier deliberation, but speed and accuracy are often at odds. Deliberation in the heat of the moment will necessarily involve fewer heads and less time to scratch them. But, after the fact, when political leaders submit to judgment, there will be plenty of time for deliberation on questions of guilt and responsibility.

---

[40] On this point, see Ian Shapiro, "Problems, Methods, and Theories in the Study of Politics, or: What's Wrong with Political Science and What To Do about It," in Shapiro, *The Flight From Reality in the Social Sciences*, pp. 178–203.

PLURALISM AND THE TROUBLES WITH EXCEPTIONALISM

Our task was to navigate between exceptionalism and strict philosophical liberalism. The aim was to avoid the dichotomy altogether by underlining the role of agency (the space between the law and its execution) in emergency measures and by showing how a plurality of values operates continuously. I have argued that the existence in a functional form of the liberal democratic state constitutes a countervailing moral value that stands as a reason in active moral decision making, and this resolves many of the conundrums that faced the norm/exception perspective. Because this framework provides for the continued force of liberal democratic norms, even in conditions where urgency and scale heighten the role of norms of order, accountability remains a possibility, or even a necessity. For the same reason, a liberal democracy might remain liberal democratic even while it exercises emergency powers.

This framework reflects the Lockean approach to emergency. First, it echoes Locke in emphasizing that the rule of individuals and the government of norms are not mutually exclusive. By allowing that principles might generate conflicting prescriptions for action, it allows that those principles might be rendered consistent through action itself. Agency has a character beyond that of rule-execution, and even beyond rule-determination. Moral agency involves deliberation also. In this way, it reaps the Lockean benefit of flexibility but retains the possibility of accountability. Locke's prerogative power, as I showed in Chapter 3, allowed for *Spielraum* bounded by an appeal to heaven. Contemporary institutional structures provide a number of options, short of violent revolution, for holding a political leader to account, but the principle is the same.

Furthermore, Locke's empirical liberalism manifests in my emphasis on the role of deliberation in mediating conflicting principles. This in turn entails the centralization of the empirical and of experience in determining the right course of action. Deliberation means taking empirical circumstances into account. A well-designed constitution minimizes crises and well-designed emergency powers meet those crises that nonetheless arise with a minimum of tragedy. Hence, a knowledge of what kinds of emergency powers optimize both efficiency and safety would seem to be a moral obligation for legislators. While there is less than we might hope in the way of sound social scientific data on emergency, the final chapter will pose some hypotheses for empirical testing that might make some small headway toward offsetting this lack.

The arguments in this chapter have also clarified the concept of necessity and the slippage between descriptive and normative exception while addressing the incoherence of the idea of a moral law subject to exception. It is now clearer what emergency powers are necessary *for*. Exercising emergency powers in the name of necessity implicitly invokes the instrumental and intrinsic value of the liberal democratic state as a moral justification. If the existence of the state in a functional form, its capacity to serve the moral aims that constitute its essence is *actually* under threat, those emergency actions that are demonstrably necessary for the restoration of order can be described as 'morally necessary' in the sense of 'means-necessity.' By making explicit what exactly is threatened and how, it becomes easier to judge the accuracy and moral weight of a statesman's reasons for emergency action.

It follows from this how an empirical description of urgent threat might be transformed into ethical information justifying emergency action. While the situation might well be 'exceptional,' exceptionality itself is neither necessary nor sufficient to justify emergency powers. It is not necessary because there are cases where urgency is the norm. It is not sufficient because exceptionality on its own provides no moral information. It is the special moral quality of an urgent threat to order that warrants emergency powers, when they are in fact warranted. Moreover, these emergency powers are not justified on the basis of an *exception* from a moral norm, but instead by means of a countervailing moral principle, that of a morally robust conception of order. There is no moral exception required and the descriptive does not slip into the normative haphazardly. Explicitness here can offset the dangers of the rhetoric of necessity and the 'exception.'

The conceptual and moral coherence of the pluralist view is also superior to the norm/exception view for the simple reason that, in admitting the existence of countervailing moral principles, rights do not cease to apply either morally or politically. Their violation remains a serious and culpable matter. What I advocate serves to contrast with those philosophers such as Kant and, more recently, Alan Donagan, who insist that ethics must ultimately provide a single, right course of action, determinable through abstract reason, and that duties, or at least perfect duties, cannot conflict.[41] The complexities of political ethics cannot be resolved into a single, consistent set of strictures that show a unified right course of action.

The pluralism I have advocated does not, by running together emergency action and normal action, 'normalize the exception,' as Schmitt infamously did. On the contrary, there can be and should be *no such thing* as a normative exception. In tempering the role of the categories of norm/exception, and by instead invoking pluralism of the kind I have described, it becomes possible to insist on the constant force and weight of liberal norms without conceding that emergency powers are immoral *tout court*. Liberal norms function always. So do norms of order.

A careful reader might caution that appeals to order as a value in political discourse may have about them an air of extreme conservativism. The idea that preserving order is a value might suggest, in general, a resistance to change, or even a moral stricture against change. Indeed, Ferejohn and Pasquino have suggested that this kind of conservativism is one of the defining features of emergency powers.[42] No order is wholly just, and so if indeed emergency powers exhibit this characteristic conservativism, it is a delicate question to what extent an order must be just before existential ethics are justified. Take, for example, the case of the General Strike of May 1926 in the United Kingdom. Many would agree that the class structure that characterized the UK of 1926 was unjust. It was a liberal democratic order with significant moral flaws. When several important industrial sectors, members of the Trade Union Congress, walked out in support of miners whose wages were about to be severely cut, the government of the United Kingdom declared a state of emergency in response, justified by their claim that the state's existence in a functional form was

---

[41] See, further, Immanuel Kant, *The Metaphysics of Morals*; Alan Donagan, *The Theory of Morality*. Kant holds that imperfect duties can conflict with perfect duties and Donagan makes an exception for situations where previous wrongdoing has generated obligations.

[42] Ferejohn and Pasquino, "The Law of Exception," p. 210.

threatened. The Government crushed the strike in six days.[43] To the extent that the workers sought to challenge the injustice of the order itself, the justice of this state of emergency is difficult to ascertain.

But there is nothing *inherently* static about the concept of order. Institutions can be altered, elections held, constitutions changed, regimes can make transitions, an order can alter in an orderly fashion. Indeed, as we shall see in Chapter 5, emergency powers have sometimes been employed effectively to facilitate peaceful social change. We could evaluate the actions of the Government of the United Kingdom on the following basis: were other means available to the strikers that had a fair chance of effecting peaceful change without resort to a general strike? If not, emergency powers would not have been justified in this case. Social conditions can and must be allowed to evolve within a political order.

This is a difficulty worthy of serious consideration, given that most every liberal democracy is in several respects unjust. It will not always be clear to political leaders when a conflict that aims at changing structural inequalities is morally sound. Where institutions can be ordered to provide nonviolent outlets for new social currents, thereby minimizing conflicts between existential and liberal ethics, we have a second order obligation to institute such measures.[44]

CONCLUSION

An empirically oriented political ethics makes possible the pluralism I have recommended. This pluralism, in turn, provides a means of overcoming the norm/exception dichotomy. We remove the dangerous carte blanche of exceptionalism, but also the knee-jerk charge of immorality, to which statesmen are likely to respond by ignoring ethics in general. Of course, this pluralism does not resolve the often tragic conflicts between values that emergency generates. On the contrary, it requires

---

[43] See Keith Jeffery and Peter Hennessy, *States of Emergency: British Governments and Strikebreaking since 1919.*

[44] Ruth Barcan Marcus, in "Moral Dilemmas and Consistency," argues that "although dilemmas are not settled without residue, the recognition of their reality has a dynamic force. It is the underpinning for a second-order regulative principle: that as rational agents with some control of our lives and institutions, we ought to conduct our lives and arrange our institutions so as to minimize predicaments of moral conflict" (p. 121).

that we continue to confront conflict as the reality of political ethics. But if we conceive of emergency powers as an extension of normal powers of order enforcement, then we provide a potential justification for their occasional use that helps us to better understand their function and place in liberal democracies. We do not rule out emergency powers, but in designing and making use of them, it becomes possible to maintain the same level of concern and the same kinds of concerns as we do under normal circumstances. Even in times of emergency, rights never cease to matter. The terms of discussion become more subtle and less liable to excess or excesses of rhetoric, and this makes emergency powers just a little bit safer.

Chapter 5 takes up the question of how we might justify mitigations of the rule of law. There, too, as we shall see, emergencies are characterized by continuity and a different kind of pluralism prevails.

5

The Rule of Law and the Roman Dictatorship

Concentration of power is a standard feature of crisis government. Because this kind of emergency provision is often conceptualized as a mitigation of the rule of law in favor of individual or arbitrary rule, here, too, norms and exceptions are a common but blunt conceptual tool. Conceptualizing the problem of emergency powers as a problem of the rule of law (normal) contra arbitrary or individual rule (exceptional) rests on the premise that this dichotomy constitutes a mutually exclusive and collectively exhaustive account of power, which implies an unwarranted solidification of power and institutions. No state is purely ruled by law. States are only more or less under the rule of law. And a state under even the most extreme constitutional emergency powers is never entirely subject to the sovereign will of an individual, as Carl Schmitt implies is possible. Institutions confer formal powers, but institutions and laws are among a number of means of constraining the informal flow of power. Hence, any normative account of emergency powers that aims at safely optimizing liberal democratic values under emergency conditions will have to set aside norms/exceptions, and instead contend with this more complex and continuous landscape of risk and enablement.

Now, the Roman dictatorship is a favorite trope of scholars of emergency government, widely cited but ill understood. It is purported to be the paradigm of this dichotomous shift to a state of exception in constitutional regimes. But a more careful examination of the Roman Dictatorship shows that the dichotomy of a rule of law that is 'normal' and an individual emergency rule that is 'exceptional' is a false one.

Instead, the Roman example illustrates that things are at once more complicated and smoother at the point of transition than a dichotomous shift from the rule of law toward individual rule would suggest. The Roman example better illustrates the continuity between normalcy and emergency, which, in turn, illustrates two senses in which an undifferentiated focus on the rule of law is misguided. First, such a focus ignores the centrality of informal power and its informal constraint. Making emergency powers safer requires that we acknowledge what is in other contexts obvious: officers inhabit offices and officers' power is not coextensive with the power of an office. While institutions confer and constrain power formally, power is constrained and enabled informally as well.

Second, the dichotomous approach, emphasizing as it does the rule of law, clouds its instrumentality. All good political institutions are instruments to moral ends. But the rule of law is neither necessary to nor sufficient for the intrinsic values it serves. If, as I argue, our concern is for the fate of these underlying values more than for the rule of law itself, then the question we should pose is rather "In times of emergency, when institutions shift to provide more flexibility and speed, how can we best further the values of uniformity and predictability in political life?" Any normative account of emergency powers that aims at safely optimizing liberal democratic values under emergency conditions will have to contend with this more complex landscape of risk and enablement. Hence, what follows is not a response to this aspect of the challenge of emergency power, but an outline of a better approach.

At stake here are both practical and conceptual matters. Conceptually, my arguments challenge the norm/exception dichotomy that dominates political thought on emergencies. The difference in the structure of power between emergency and normal circumstances is of degree and not of kind. In practical terms, when power is concentrated under emergency provisions our concern should be with enablement and constraint more generally, both formal and informal, and not simply with the rule of law.

EMERGENCY RULE AND THE RULE OF LAW

For the purposes of this chapter, I draw on Dicey and Hayek in stipulating a rough definition of the rule of law.[1] A state is under the rule of law if its source of coercion is not an individual but a set of rules that are universally applicable and enforceable, and publicly promulgated. Such rules constitute the formal enablement and constraint of power. That is to say, a state is under the rule of law if political actors' power is coextensive with the enablements and goes no further than the constraints specifically described by the rules. Formally delineated rules give power and power is checked by formal rules.

That the rule of law must be universally applicable necessitates rules that are general, and it has historically been a defining feature of arbitrary government that individuals can be made subject to coercive rules specific to themselves. Publicly promulgating the rules serves the purpose of facilitating predictability, while openness helps prevent corruption. It is easier to enforce universality if the rules are universally known.

Since Aristotle, political thinkers have recognized that law's generality must, on certain occasions, conflict with justice.[2] This is sometimes called the problem of equity: the equal application of the law may sometimes be unjust, as when a first offense is treated more leniently. Problems of equity concern tensions between generality and particularity and in this respect, emergency is its close relation. Here, too, the issue is one of unforeseeable or descriptively exceptional cases, where application of the laws might result in injustice. For this reason, many theorists recommend a suspension or alteration of the rules and a shift in institutional structure in times of crisis to accommodate the requirement of speed and to circumvent the inflexibility of the rule of law. Individual rule and individual judgment, in place of the rule of law, become a necessity. As we saw in Chapter 2, in

---

[1] F. W. Hayek, *The Constitution of Liberty*. p. 153ff, p. 210ff; A. V. Dicey, *Introduction to the Study of the Law of the Constitution*, p. 114ff. As with all terms of art in political theory, the rule of law could be defined in a cluster of different ways. See, e.g., Ian Shapiro (ed.), *The Rule of Law*. See also Richard Fallon, "'The Rule of Law' as a Concept in Constitutional Discourse."

[2] Aristotle, *The Politics*, e.g. pp. 1282b, 1286a. But see also *Nichomachean Ethics*, p. 1138a.

their different ways Rousseau, Machiavelli, and Hamilton[3] have all come out strongly in favor of increased *Spielraum* for the executive in times of urgency, and Locke tells us: "Many things there are, which the law can by no means provide for, and those must necessarily be left to the discretion of him, that has executive power in his hands."[4] Law has its limits.

Emergency conditions are usually urgent conditions and the deliberate element of law making in deliberative democracies makes the rule of those laws steady and sedate. The slow creation of law aims specifically at precluding hasty decision making, on the understanding that speed often results in error whereas deliberation involves care, attention, and consideration of diverse perspectives and interests. The great lag between the development of a policy and the coming into force of a law shows why, under urgent conditions, some more expedient means of decision making might be desirable. Indeed, in practice, concentration of power and limitation of rights characterize the emergency powers of nearly every country, including strong liberal democracies like the United States (Article 1, s. 9 c.2),[5] France (Article 16), and Germany (Articles 115a, 115d). These provisions minimize checks and balances and reduce decision time. The rule of law is curtailed. Regardless of good laws, regardless even of good dispositions to make laws, law cannot rule alone. This is true even in everyday government, where discretion and flexibility come in at every stage. Public officials exercise discretion regarding which laws are considered, when laws are enforced, and what ought to be done when the law is silent.[6]

We might think that granting such discretion to political leaders in times of crisis and otherwise poses a challenge to liberalism's foundational concern with the prevention of domination through the limitation of arbitrary power. If the rule of law is a central element of liberalism,

---

[3] On Hamilton particularly, see also Clement Fatovic, "Constitutionalism and Presidential Prerogative: Jeffersonian and Hamiltonian Perspectives."

[4] John Locke, *Second Treatise of Government*, s. 159. Recent discussions of Locke's prerogative powers include Vicente Medina, "Locke's Militant Liberalism"; Clement Fatovic, "Constitutionalism and Contingency: Locke's Theory of Prerogative"; and Pasquale Pasquino, "Locke on King's Prerogative."

[5] Abraham Lincoln famously made use of this power in 1861 and 1862 at the beginning of the American Civil War.

[6] On this see Lazar, "A Topography of Emergency Power," in Victor V. Ramraj (ed.), *The Rule of Law in Time of Crisis.*

and if emergency powers involve its suspension, then they might be inherently illiberal, their existence a matter of normative and conceptual concern. Indeed, a number of scholars have come out very strongly against emergency measures on just such grounds.[7] But discretion is in fact quite normal. In responding to the very real dangers and tensions of emergency powers our focus should be broader. Emergency powers are not illiberal in mitigating the rule of law, because it is not the rule of law itself but the values underlying it that are intrinsically valuable. Hence, the rule of law is not necessary to liberal government unless it should turn out that it is instrumentally necessary. Furthermore, because power is not delimited by its formal enablement and constraint, the rule of law is not sufficient either.

We can explain the rule of law's importance with reference to underlying substantive values. In many academic accounts, the rule of law is tied to liberty, equality, and dignity. Hayek, for example, has argued that its generality protects individuals from arbitrary persecution.[8] Assuring the capacity of individuals to predict when and how they might come under the sway of the law enables a sphere of liberty. Dicey underlines the inherent equality of the rule of law. Everyone is subjected to the same body of law and procedure, no less those who govern than those who are governed.[9] And for Rawls, uniformity and predictability are central to the autonomous pursuit of personal aims.[10]

In each case, the value of the rule of law is delineated by reference to more fundamental values: it serves the aims of predictability and uniformity, which in turn serve liberty and equality. We value the rule of law not in itself, not as intrinsically valuable, but rather for what it brings.

If we understand the rule of law in this way, we leave open the possibility that these values might be furthered in some other way. Should

---

[7] Among the many examples are Lee Epstein et al., "The Effect of War on the Supreme Court," p. 6; William Scheuerman, "Rethinking Crisis Government"; Diane P. Wood, "The Rule of Law in Times of Stress."

[8] Hayek, *Constitution of Liberty*, pp. 153–4.

[9] Dicey, *Introduction to the Law of the Constitution*, p. 114.

[10] John Rawls, *A Theory of Justice*, p. 235. Robert Nozick has also underlined the centrality of the rule of law, for example in the slave thought experiment in his *Anarchy, State, and Utopia*, p. 290ff.

circumstances arise in which the rule of law was counterproductive or less effective than some alternative, we would be justified in making the relevant shifts: the rule of law is not normatively necessary unless it should turn out that it is instrumentally necessary.

Furthermore, because the rule of law focuses our attention on the formal aspects of power, there are good reasons to think it is also insufficient for promoting and preserving the values of uniformity and predictability for the sake of liberty and equality. This focus on formal power is evident both among those who revile it and those who are content to concentrate authority in emergencies. For Carl Schmitt, for example, the very idea of a sovereign dictatorship rests on the assumption that there could be an office, the holder of which exercised complete existential control, beyond formal constraint.[11] Politics has no real place in such a pantheon. Power is unidirectional. For liberal thinkers, in an equal but opposite way, law is conceived of as the formal regulator of power, the force that grants and obstructs it. Both for those who support and for those who oppose the suspension of the rule of law, a linear, Weberian conception of power is at work. The state has a monopoly on the legitimate use of force, and that force is delineated by specific formal legal mechanisms. Schmitt's concept of sovereignty and his understanding of the political are reliant on this notion. And so, in an equal but opposite way, is the understanding of liberal emergency theorists such as Bill Scheuerman. For both, law stands in opposition to sovereign power.

But this formal conceptualization of power leaves out a central and otherwise obvious factor: the informal contest over power engendered in politics. In a crisis, the informal enablement and constraint of power are at least as important as the formal aspects embodied in the rule of law. They can enable political leaders to disregard or abuse the values underlying the rule of law, even while observing the letter of the law. They can also prevent abuses and provide alternative constraints in the absence of a strict rule of law regime. Hence, if we want to make emergency powers safer, we would do well to take note of this broader political landscape.

[11] See, generally, Carl Schmitt, *Die Diktatur*; see also *Political Theology*, p. 5ff.

THE DICTATORSHIP IN REPUBLICAN ROME

In explaining this central importance of informal aspects of power in emergencies, I want to begin with an illustration. Its significance is not in any wholly novel discovery about this institution based on new archaeological or textual information. Instead, it illustrates a more fundamental point. In the process, it serves to show how easily, particularly in the study of the ancient world, historical accounts can be bent to political purposes.

Both those who have wished to praise the suspension of the rule of law in emergencies and those who have found it worrisome have tended to make their case with reference to the Roman Dictatorship. Political theorists have found in the dictatorship of the Early and Middle Republic exactly those features seemingly necessary to the management of emergency circumstances in constitutional and rule of law regimes: speed, decisiveness, exception from the normal legal order, personal authority in place of the rule of law.[12] Thus, there is no more suitable way of illustrating this broader landscape of power and its constraint and the fallacious nature of the dichotomous conception of arbitrary rule and the rule of law than through a careful account of this very institution. It serves as a clear illustration of the complex conception of power and constraint and as a counterexample to the more dichotomous norm/exception rule of law/individual rule conception it is normally used to illustrate. And, while important differences separate the Roman and the contemporary case, the structure of the problem and the principles with which we might confront it are not so far apart.

---

[12] It is important to note that we in fact know very little with certainty about this institution, or any other of the Early or Middle Republic. Classicists accept that the literary accounts we have are at least partly fictitious, or at least so politically motivated that it would be irresponsible to take them as plainly factual. Later thinkers madly embellished and selectively reproduced earlier accounts. But even Livy and Dionysius, our so-called primary sources, were up to those same tricks, at least to some extent. Occasionally, archaeological evidence can help in this regard, but since such evidence is sketchy, my account is not strictly intended to provide definitive, new, historical insight into the institution of dictatorship itself, but rather illustrates its 'use and abuse.' Instead, what these early writers and our documentary evidence suggest comes from what these authors find not worth noting. If these common and significant deviations from our usual trope seem to serve no political purpose for early authors, and if other aspects of the historical record tally up, then this is enough to prompt questions about the modern trope. A definitive account is not necessary to this end. It is enough to show that the trope is a late construction.

We should take care at the outset to distinguish this institution from its Late Republic and twentieth-century namesakes. The Roman Dictatorship of the Early and Middle Republic was a formally limited, frequent but intermittent, and constitutional office. In the dying days of the Republic, Caesar and Sulla subverted the institution by removing its formal limitation. While constitutional innovation was common in Republican Rome, this went well beyond the common understanding of the spirit of the office, and the dictatorships of Caesar and Sulla are institutionally separate from, even if parasitic upon, those of earlier periods.[13] The more recent subversion invests in a single individual complete and continuous formal control over every aspect of the state. As should be clear from this discussion, this form of government has more in common with the late dictatorships than with those under consideration here, and, even then, these forms of dictatorship share little in common beyond the literal element of command.

Our interest rests with the emergency institution used by the Romans of the Early and Middle republican periods. With this form of dictatorship, the Romans could concentrate power to manage exigencies within the context of their complex and carefully rule- and tradition-bound constitution.[14] But the differing ideological perspectives of ancient and contemporary historians, the lack of trustworthy early sources, and the unwritten and evolving character of the Roman constitution have meant that the range of the dictator's powers are a matter of continuing contention. Under the circumstances, the dictator trope in the history of political thought since Machiavelli has been surprisingly uniform. In a nutshell, this trope invokes the following claim: the dictator could do anything at all to advance the task he had been set except change the constitution. Machiavelli claims that he could act without consultation and punish without appeal, but that he could not change existing institutions.[15] Rousseau concurs: "He can

---

[13] An interesting account of the transition is found in Claude Nicolet, "Le Dictature à Rome," recently translated as "Dictatorship in Rome," in Peter Baehr and Melvin Richter (eds.), *Dictatorship in History and Theory*, pp. 263–78.

[14] The Roman constitution more closely resembled the British than the American constitution, insofar as duties and entitlements as well as structures and procedures of government were specified in a number of separated laws and in unwritten custom, or *mos maiorum*.

[15] Machiavelli, *Discourses*, I.34–5.

do anything except make laws."[16] Schmitt stresses his freedom from legal restrictions and attributes to him "unlimited power over life and death."[17] Rossiter insists that, with the exception of the law-making restriction, the dictator's powers were boundless; he became "as absolute a ruler as could well be imagined."[18] Richard Posner compares the Roman dictator to a Hitler or a Stalin.[19] And Oren Gross claims that "he alone was free from any intercession by the tribunes and from senatorial intervention and direction . . . [and] the dictator's authority did not extend to the promulgation of new legislation."[20]

None of these claims is true, strictly speaking.[21] The dictator's power was importantly limited both formally and informally, and, in fact, through the acquisition of informal power, several dictators succeeded in legislating, and even altering the constitution, usually to the benefit of the plebeians.[22] To see how and why this was so, we should begin with a brief overview of the complexities of Roman government.[23] By showing the power structure in which the dictatorships were situated, how it was enabled and constrained, we can see both the continuity in normal and exceptional power and the necessity of

[16] Rousseau, *Du contrat social*, IV. 6.

[17] Schmitt, *Die Diktatur*, 1. My translation.

[18] Clinton Rossiter, *Constitutional Dictatorship*, p. 23.

[19] Richard Posner, *Not a Suicide Pact*, p. 68.

[20] Oren Gross, "The Concept of 'Crisis': What Can We Learn from the Two Dictatorships of L. Quinctius Cincinnatus?" pp. 1–2.

[21] At this point, I wish to explain why I am concentrating on later sources in addition to drawing on the work of Livy, Plutarch, etc. There are so many inconsistencies between ancient historical accounts that it is difficult to take any of them as authoritative. A contemporary study that examines claims against a broader range of evidence, not all of which would have been available to ancient authors, presents an attractive alternative. My main source on the dictatorship is therefore Marianne Hartfield, "The Roman Dictatorship: Its Character and Its Evolution." Hartfield presents evidence from a range of sources, including extant laws and *fasti*, and compares accounts in Livy, Dionysius of Halicarnassus, Plutarch, etc., providing a detailed account of every instance of dictatorship in the Roman Republic.

[22] An anonymous referee has suggested that the relationship of the word 'dictator' and the verb '*dico*,' meaning both 'to order' and 'to speak,' suggests the dictator's capacity to legislate. However, an order can constitute an act of *execution* as well as an act of *legislation*. Still, the point is worth noting insofar as later dictators, such as Hitler, invoked word as law *tout court*.

[23] My account of the Roman constitution draws on Andrew Lintott, *The Constitution of the Roman Republic*; and Hans Julius Wolff, *Roman Law: An Historical Introduction*.

going beyond rule of law rhetoric to evaluate the safety and potential of emergency powers in a liberal democratic context.

Rome had three primary centers of power, the senate, the magistrates, and the people. It also had three kinds of power: *auctoritas* (authority, or advisory capacity in matters requiring judgment), *potestas* (capacity, efficacy, force), and *imperium* (supreme administrative or coercive power).[24]

The senate's roots are found in a king's council. Its members were men of political experience, chosen by a consul or by a dictator.[25] The senate's power was *auctoritas* with which it played a number of nebulous constitutional roles. Roughly, it was responsible for advising the magistrates, for holding the public purse strings, and, since it was a stable locus for petition, for conducting foreign policy. The senate would advise and mediate between magistrates and while there was no constitutional necessity that a magistrate take senatorial advice, de facto, through custom and social prestige, the senate was highly influential and difficult to oppose.[26] Yet, that the will of the senate, which numbered several hundred, was rarely uniform provided a popular means for magistrates to circumvent it. This was true of dictators too: Quinctius Cincinnatus, dictator in 439 B.C., was particularly skilled at playing the senate against itself when forced to engage in novel dictatorial activities.[27]

The magistracy was made up of executive officers tasked with carrying out the daily functions of the state. They ranked from the dictator on high, who was appointed only periodically, to the censors, whose tasks were to take a census every fifth year and to serve as governors of public morals by assigning citizens to classes.[28] In

---

[24] Perhaps a similarly diverse array of concepts in English-language political theory might reduce our tendency to oversimplify the diversity of modes of power.

[25] In the later Republic, the task of choosing senators fell to the censors, and worthy plebeians came to be eligible. Even then, however, political experience was difficult to acquire without family connections, and so patricians continued to dominate the senate.

[26] Wolff, *Roman Law*, p. 43.

[27] Cincinnatus was tasked with judging the 'conspirator' Maelius. See Hartfield, "The Roman Dictatorship," p. 71. Or see the dramatic account in Livy, *The History of Rome since Its Foundation*, IV.14.

[28] This strange double duty shows the origin of the relationship between our word 'census' for counting people and our word 'censor' for enforcing clean expression.

between were the consuls, whose many duties, judicial, military, and political, included commanding the armies and conducting elections. There were two of these, and each could veto the other if he doubted his colleague's course of action. Under normal conditions, the consuls held the fort, so to speak.

Magistrates wielded two types of power. *Potestas* gave them license to conduct their duties, which were limited by task, by law, and then further limited by any one of a number of vetoes, including those of a colleague in office, a higher magistrate, or a tribune of the plebs. *Imperium* gave a magistrate power over the bodies of the people. A dictator was not the only magistrate with *imperium* but his was highest: no magistrate, and, in the earliest years of the office, not even the people, could veto his decisions. He could compel citizens to go to war and, until the establishment of the right of *provocatio ad populum*,[29] could punish them corporally or capitally on the battlefield. While *potestas* enabled specific administrative functions, *imperium* provided a wider scope for discretion.

All magistrates, except the dictator, were elected by the citizens of Rome.[30] In addition, by the early fifth century B.C., the people were accorded political representation through the tribunes, whom they elected each year. While tribunes were not magistrates and did not wield *imperium*, neither were they subject to magistrates' *imperium*. Instead, they wielded a veto over all these others, including, late in the Republic, the dictator.[31]

Now, all these vetoes and checks form an impressive but impressively cumbersome government machinery. It is for this reason that Rome used its emergency powers so often. The dictatorship complemented and overcame the deliberate and ponderous nature of Rome's

---

[29] According to this right, only the people of Rome could sentence a citizen to death.

[30] Elections were not based on entirely democratic principles. Higher magistrates were elected by the *comitia centuriata*, a body formed through principles of military rank. Hence wealthier citizens, who could afford better equipment, and therefore a more distinguished role in battle, were accorded more votes. Lower magistrates were appointed by the *comitia tributa*, which represented districts. There is at least one recorded case of a dictator being elected: in 217 B.C., with one consul dead and another trapped in battle, the *comitia tributa* were called upon to elect a dictator, and chose Q. Fabius Maximus.

[31] Wolff, *Roman Law*, p. 37.

normal institutions. But it, like Rome's other institutions, existed within a web of formal and informal constraint and enablement.

The Roman Dictatorship formed an integral part of the republican constitution almost from its beginning, continuing in frequent use through the fifth and fourth centuries, and then declining throughout the third century until administrative and military considerations led it into dormancy after 202 B.C. Its flexibility stemmed from the fact that "*mos* not *lex* restrained the Dictator's performance."[32] The original and most important role for a dictator was military but many later dictators were called by the senate for a number of nonmilitary tasks as well.[33] Military dictatorships were designated *rei gerundae causa* (*rgc*) which literally means, 'to get things done.'

Much is made by both ancient and modern authors of another kind of dictatorship – *seditionis sedandae* (*ss*), to put down civil insurrections. On this basis, Livy, for instance, sometimes claims that the dictatorship was a tool of the senate against the plebs, while Dionysius of Halicarnassus also underlines its importance in maintaining social order.[34] However, Livy elsewhere agrees with Cicero that the dictatorship's central function was as a unified command in war.[35] Indeed dictators passed popular legislation against the wishes of the senate more often than they put down popular uprisings. There were ninety-four dictatorships in Republican Rome, of which only four served to put down popular uprisings, despite near constant civil strife. Nonetheless, conducting foreign wars and striving for local peace were sometimes not strictly separable. Legal concessions to the plebs helped in raising armies, which in turn could help the dictator fulfill the military

---

[32] Hartfield, "The Roman Dictatorship," p. 124.

[33] Hartfield, "The Roman Dictatorship," p. 17ff.

[34] Livy, *The History of Rome*, 2.18; Dionysius of Halicarnassus, *The Roman Antiquities*, 5.63–76. Gross stresses this role of the dictatorship as though it were a nasty outgrowth of its original 'external affairs' oriented purpose. However, there is good reason to think that, for the Romans, the functions of 'internal' and 'external' would not have been strictly separate in this regard in the first place. The dictator was a pseudo-king, not a wielder of Lockean 'federative power.' There is no evidence that dictatorships *ss* constituted a 'subversion' of the original function of the dictatorship. See, generally, Oren Gross, "The Concept of 'Crisis.'"

[35] Livy, *The War with Hannibal*, 23.23; Cicero, *The Republic and the Laws*, "The Laws," 3.3.9; "The Republic," 1.63.

task he had been set. In other cases, raising an army could require more direct dictatorial intervention.[36]

After 376 B.C., dictators fulfilled a number of consular functions if a consul was unavailable or incapacitated: they held elections or ceremonial games, and chose new senators (before this became a duty of the censors). Dictators also fulfilled religious and symbolic functions such as hammering a nail into the Capitoline temple to cure a plague (*clavi figendi causa*) and reading the auspices.[37] Given this variety of dictatorial duties, it will come as no surprise that, in the 300 years between the first recorded appointment of a dictator, T. Larcius Flavus, in 501 B.C. and the last proper appointment, that of C. Servillius, in 202 B.C., a dictator was appointed approximately once every three years, for up to six months.

Typically, a dictatorship would be instituted in the following manner. The senate would decide that a dictator was necessary, and a consul would appoint one. This process prevented the senate from choosing one of its own, although a consul often did choose a senator. Dictators were nearly always prominent men who had demonstrated their ability and their trustworthiness. One man could serve as dictator on multiple occasions. Furius Camillus, for example, was made dictator no less than

---

[36] Cicero, "The Republic," 1.73. "Social tensions, class rivalries and struggles, especially manifested by plebeian refusals to serve in the armies, occasionally influenced the Senate's turn to the Dictatorship...[but on those occasions] the social turmoil was not of recent origin. The senate had resisted plebeian pressures for some time without considering the Dictatorship." It was, apparently, only the emergence of an imminent military threat that prompted this action. Lintott has speculated about these different understandings of the relationship of the dictatorship to the plebs on the basis of an author's political stance: "as with many uncertain constitutional issues, the different positions that could be taken reflected either an aristocratic, authoritarian ideology or one that was popular and libertarian." See Andrew Lintott, *The Constitution of the Roman Republic*, p. 112.

[37] In times of plague, a dictator would be appointed to literally hammer a nail into the Capitoline Temple. The origin of this strange function is recorded in Livy (*The History of Rome*, VI, 2). A plague having preyed upon Rome for some years, and other means of appeasement having failed "the older men remembered (so it is said) that at one time an outbreak of plague had been reduced by the Dictator's hammering the nail," which used to be done to mark the year. Thereafter, a dictator was always appointed for this purpose, and he would always abdicate immediately afterward. It is interesting that even in these nonmilitary cases, the dictator would appoint a "master of the horse." This would seem to suggest that the military stature of the dictator was part of what suggested his dignity and power, and therefore part of what would make his action pleasing in the eyes of the gods.

five times.[38] The dictator was set a specific task, and then he would appoint a deputy, who was called *magister equitum*, or master of the horse.[39] Generally, the whole preliminary process could be concluded in a day or two. The dictator could then quickly set out to war or to hammering nails, running elections, and so on.

The responsibilities of dictators *rgc* were often confined to a specific geographical area. In the Early Republic, this was almost always outside Rome but later, the senate occasionally gave an additional, domestic *senatus consultum* to a dictator in office before he abdicated. In any case, a dictator who successfully trounced an enemy would often return to 'triumph' and it was not unusual for a dictator to continue in his role within Rome's boundaries until these celebrations were concluded and his obligations to the gods fulfilled.[40] Upon completion of his task, or after six months (whichever came first), the dictator would formally set down his powers and resume his civilian life.[41]

I noted earlier that political thinkers concur that a Dictator's authority was bounded only by the requirement that he fulfill his task or lay down his power within a set time, and the requirement that he not change the constitution. I also suggested that neither of these claims is accurate. Because of the presence of informal constraints and enablements, the dictator's power was both broader and narrower than is commonly ascribed. It illustrates a smoother transition between normal and exceptional political circumstances.

There are records of seven dictators who passed legislation, roughly 7.5 percent of all dictators, including those appointed for simple

---

[38] Furius Camillus served in the years 396, 390, 386, 368, and 367 B.C. He brought Rome a series of spectacular victories, especially against the Gauls. The year 368 was an exception. In that year, Furius Camillus resigned after one frantic day in office because of a debacle. He had attempted to cow rather than coopt the plebeians: a disastrous strategy in this case.

[39] It is interesting to note that the Dictator himself was strictly associated with the infantry.

[40] A Roman triumph was a special public celebration to glorify a successful military leader. A dictator might then repay the gods for victory with things gods were thought to enjoy: ceremonial games, statues, temple dedications, etc.

[41] There was at least one case of a dictator staying on for up to a year and then passing power over to another dictator. But this was extremely rare and dictated by geographical military complications.

ceremonial tasks.[42] Some of the laws in question altered the structure of the government significantly and all but one were significant achievements for the plebeians in the face of senatorial opposition. For example, the dictator of 367 B.C., M. Furius Camillus, promulgated a law establishing that a plebeian could hold one of the consulships. M. Aemilius Mamercinus, appointed Dictator *rgc* in 434 B.C. to trample an expected Etruscan uprising – which never materialized – took the opportunity to pass a popular law, the *lex Aemilia de censura minuenda* or law shortening the duration of the censorship (from 5 years to 18 months). The law was proposed to and overwhelmingly approved by the popular *comitia tributa* and strongly opposed by the senate. It is noteworthy that "no one . . . complained or hinted that Aemilius acted illegally."[43]

Thus, it appears that a dictator could and did legislate, and indeed even alter the constitution, particularly when it served the public interest or appeased the people. Such actions both required and cemented public support, which might well have been necessary to fulfill broader military tasks. Both show the potential importance of popularity in achieving political as well as military aims, which suggests that this functioned as an informal means of enabling a dictator to engage in circumscribed activities and also of constraining him from engaging in certain others. The dictator could act as a sort of vanguard, as long as he had reason to expect popular support.[44]

The second claim, that the dictator could do anything related to his task, that indeed, in Rossiter's words, the dictator was "as absolute a ruler as could well be imagined," is also untrue.[45] This seems a strange way to describe a man who could not even mount a horse without

---

[42] The dictators who legislated for plebeian benefit, but not on constitutional matters, included: Valerius Corvus, whose *lex Valeria militaris* provided mutinous soldiers amnesty and lowered the cavalry's pay, while a further law forbade military tribunes from becoming centurion commanders; and Manlius Capitolinus, dictator *ss* and *rgc* in 368 B.C. who, according to Plutarch, passed a law that limited the possession of public land, for purposes of redistribution. See Hartfield, "Roman Dictatorship," pp. 276–9.

[43] Hartfield, "Roman Dictatorship," p. 277.

[44] This contradicts Ferejohn and Pasquino's recent claim in "The Law of Exception" that emergency powers in general and the dictatorship in particular are inherently conservative insofar as they aim to restore the status quo. There is no reason, in theory at least, why the same vaguely vanguardist principles governing restorative emergency powers could not also govern regime transition. See, e.g., pp. 210–12.

[45] Rossiter, *Constitutional Dictatorship*, p. 23.

permission.[46] Rossiter lists, startlingly blind to their significance, a wide range of formal and informal restrictions with which the dictator must contend. For money he was reliant on the senate, his term was limited, he could do little without popular support, he had no civil judicial power, and he could not himself decide to launch an offensive war.

By 363 B.C., the dictator came under the tribune's veto as surely as any other magistrate,[47] and by 300 B.C. the *provocatio ad populum* joined the list of restrictions on his power. Indeed, Lintott has argued from evidence in Livy and in extant text of the law itself that the *lex repetundarum* allows for a dictator and his *magister equitum* to be charged on abdication if they overstepped while in office.

Furthermore, although other magistrates were held in abeyance while the dictator was in Rome, there is no reason to think that the senate's power was reduced, except voluntarily. Machiavelli, at least, clearly recognizes the continuation of the customary effect of the senate's prestige and social standing. And Rossiter does recognise that "the 'advice' of the Senate was rarely disregarded by any Roman official" but strangely accords it no significance.[48] Hartfield cites numerous instances of the senate issuing a *senatus consultum* that a dictator promptly followed. This seems to have been the most usual course, and, although the senate wielded an imperfect *auctoritas*, as we can see from the laws passed against its official wishes, it is clear that dictators only occasionally strayed beyond their original task without a *senatus consultum* to back them up.[49]

In a different vein, the structure of informal incentives heavily favored good behavior on the part of dictators. For example, holding the dictatorship was rarely the last post in a person's public career. Men could be appointed dictator on multiple occasions, and many ran for consul after serving as dictator. The patriotic impulse and "religious aura of the office"[50] bolstered the political necessity of appearing honorable.

[46] Lintott cites Cicero, Livy, Festus, Plutarch, and others in support of this claim. *The Constitution of the Roman Republic*, p. 110.

[47] This was the case with L. Manlius Imperiosus who, as Dictator *Clavi Figendi Causa* in 363 B.C., decided hammering a nail was a dull way to pass his time as dictator and set about other tasks, until the tribunes put a stop to it. Livy, *The History of Rome*, VI.2ff.

[48] Rossiter, *Constitutional Dictatorship*, p. 19.

[49] Hartfield, "Roman Dictatorship," pp. 48, 49, 55.

[50] Hartfield, "Roman Dictatorship," p. 24.

Some of these constraints are formal, such as the later vetoes and the *provocatio*, but many are of a powerfully informal nature, such as electoral incentives and reliance on the senate for advice, approval, and funds. That Rossiter considers a figure subject to these constraints, which he calls 'minor,' to be as absolute a ruler as could well be imagined is nothing short of astonishing.[51]

Just as the informal power of popular support enabled unusual measures such as the passing of a law, so informal incentives and disincentives and informal power flows restricted dictators' activities. Freed from the encumbrance of so many vetoes, the dictator was still enmeshed in a web of political influence and incentives that contributed to and bounded his power in various ways. The overall structure of incentives and disincentives, of constraints and enablements was continuous across normal and emergency government, and it is this that must be considered in evaluating the safety and effectiveness of institutions. As with every Roman office, the extent to which the *law* guides the dictator is one factor only.

Thus, this institution was far from Rossiter's constitutional dictatorship and further still from the commissarial dictator advocated by the early Carl Schmitt. In the Early and Middle Roman Republic, there was significant continuity between the flow of power under normal and exceptional conditions. That there was a dictator did not in the slightest entail that a Schmittian *Ausnahmezustand* obtained. Instead, the Roman case illustrates that even under emergency conditions, while institutions confer power on office holders, power also exists and is harnessed in all kinds of extra-institutional ways. Extra-institutional coercion and influence provide means of skirting law or influencing its creation; there is more than one currency in politics.

---

[51] Some might question whether the awesome power of Caesar and Sulla might not constitute such absolute rule, but insofar as their power stemmed from charisma and military might, this serves more as evidence for, rather than against my claims. For, if the office of the dictatorship itself bestowed such power, if it were the power of the *office* rather than personal power, one would have expected every dictator to be equally powerful. It is in part because of the inversion of the relative importance of office and office holder in these cases that we are concerned, here, only with the Early and Middle Republic.

INFORMAL POWER AND ITS INFORMAL CONSTRAINT

Law outlines the duties and capacities of an office, emergency or otherwise. Yet, the power of the office holder and the power of the office are not coextensive. Influence and authority can come from charisma, from existing personal power, from family connections, from wealth. By virtue of the prestige and honor that an office bestows, as well as by virtue of an officer's capacity to bring about desirable states of affairs, that officer comes to wield personal power as well. Institutions and offices are created and populated by humans with agency; attention to institutional structures alone or concern for the rule of law alone is insufficient to confront the dangers and possibilities of emergency powers. To think otherwise is to reify institutions in an unwarranted fashion.

Ian Shapiro has described this focus on institutional power as a classical feature of liberalism in opposition to a republicanism that conceives of power as something over which and with which different segments of a population clash and compete.[52] Of course, in contemporary liberal democracies, institutions matter also and we must take account of both. This is in some sense obvious, but it is all too commonly overlooked in discussions of the safety of emergency powers.

With this recognition of the limited scope of the rule of law and of the continuity between modes of enablement and constraint we can return to the question of the compatibility of emergency powers with liberalism. In liberal democracies, as in the Roman Republic, emergency powers need not represent a conceptually or normatively troubling switch from rule of law to arbitrary rule. Rather, the web of formal and informal power can shift. While normal formal constraints may be weakened, there is no reason in principle or, under decent conditions, in practice why informal constraints cannot be engineered to pick up some of the slack. The key, then, is not simply to ensure the maintenance of the rule of law but to consider how power can best be constrained from violating the underlying values of uniformity and predictability while the power structure shifts in a manner conducive to effective action. Ultimately, we should evaluate institutions in their broader sociopolitical context. Conversely,

---

[52] Ian Shapiro, *The State of Democratic Theory*, p. 7.

however, we must recognize that charisma and individual political skill can supersede even the most genius constitutional thinking. Caesar and Sulla were both able to cloak their activities in legitimacy by employing the title of dictator when it was obsolete but still in accordance with the rule of law.

Nonetheless, I do not mean to suggest that the rule of law is irrelevant. Given the right informal conditions, the rule of law is instrumentally effective at constraining executive excess. We value the rule of law so highly because, given the right *informal* conditions, it can be effective at furthering the underlying values of uniformity and predictability in the service of liberty, equality, and dignity. The rule of law has instrumental value for a reason. My aim has been to underline the limitations of a perspective grounded in a dichotomy between arbitrary, individual government and the rule of law because the latter is neither absolutely necessary nor is it sufficient for safety. Its mitigation warrants caution, but is not, in itself, a crisis. Safety requires a broader perspective.

Just as power flows informally, so there are many extra-institutional means of constraining and limiting the arbitrary exercise of power. In addition, institutions themselves have constraining externalities that are informal. Here are some examples of important informal constraints, some institutionally grounded and others not, adapted from the Roman case. While it would be foolish to assume that these constraints will always obtain or to rely on them entirely, these might offset some of the danger in concentrating power during emergencies.

First, there is conscience and honor. Politicians are raised within the same civic sphere as other citizens. There is no reason to expect that a sense of the bounds of decency and a baseline of honorable conduct are not instilled just as much in politicians as they are in other citizens. This is to say, not necessarily entirely, but probably basically. A healthy civic society with a strong tradition of collective values has this mechanism as a primary constraint against gross abuse of emergency powers. Few of us could imagine grossly abusing such powers if they were in our hands, and this is likely true of most politicians as well. A complete collapse given the opportunity of emergency powers would be dependent on catastrophic preconditions. Unfortunately, strongly held civic ideals are not something a state can easily or quickly cultivate or control. Furthermore, incremental incursions, small assaults on fundamental values might be comparatively easy to stomach, and such incursions have a habit of becoming permanent.[53]

Second, there is electoral success. Even if a particular politician is less morally upright than the average citizen, the fact of the average voter's civic awareness means that, for the sake of reelection and a continuation of public status, politicians will endeavor to *appear* honorable, which means behaving within the bounds of the appearance of honor. In addition to the prestige the office grants, its publicity also extracts a duty of honorable conduct that helps to determine the prestige, honor, and hence potential power of the office holder after leaving the office in question. This is particularly true with respect to office holders who hope to progress to further offices, but it is also true of those who wish to take on another public role, or simply to be remembered favorably.

Third, there is the likelihood of detection. When emergency action is secret, as sometimes it is prone to be, this would obviously tell against reelection as an informal impetus to good behavior.[54] A civic society that fosters openness through a strong opposition and a free press with, for example, quasi nongovernmental organization watchdogs for good measure will bolster a politician's scrupulousness with respect to public image. Because the press and the opposition are easily cowed during states of emergency, a post hoc mechanism may be necessary. The certainty of a subsequent public inquiry provides a good set of incentives and constraints when emergency powers are in effect. The knowledge that ultimately one will be subject to international standards of emergency conduct, for instance in jurisdictions like the European Union where such standards (which are admittedly formal) are enforceable, can provide additional backing.[55]

---

[53] See Oren Gross and Fionnuala Ní Aoláin, *Law in Times of Crisis: Emergency Powers in Theory and Practice*, ch. 4.

[54] See Simon Chesterman, "Deny Everything: Intelligence Activities and the Rule of Law," in Victor V. Ramraj (ed.), *Emergencies and the Limits of Legality*, pp. 313–33.

[55] There is admittedly some dispute with respect to the extent to which the European Court is effective. See Christoph Schreuer, "Derogation of Human Rights in Situations of Public Emergency: The Experience of the European Convention on Human Rights." Gross and Ní Aoláin claim, on the contrary, that, after the fact, the courts tend to be supportive of the executive in countries with normally democratic institutions, and suspicious of those without. This is *potentially* consistent with Schreuer's claim that *before* the fact executives may somewhat temper their behavior. *Law in Times of Crisis*, ch. 5.

Fourth is the availability of funds. Very little can be done without money, so whoever holds the purse strings, within or outside government, also holds tremendous informal influence.

A wise regime takes as much account of these and many other informal constraints and institutional externalities as of the rule of law in the design of its emergency powers. Whatever quarrel one may have with the institutional recommendations of Bruce Ackerman (e.g., his super-majoritarian escalator), for instance, there is no denying that, to the extent they would work, they would work because they take into account informal power.[56] When individuals comply, we should look to the full landscape of constraint, both formal and informal, to understand why. Formal rules alone do not compel compliance and, to the extent that there are other means of constraining power, the rule of law is not a *necessary* condition of safety.

That so much that constrains or enables the flow of power is extra-institutional shows that the rule of law is not the *only* means of checking power. Yet it also shows that putatively sovereign power can be checked. The conception of sovereign individual power that Carl Schmitt advocates and so many others dread or admire is also too narrow. No dictator is above politics and not even the Roman Dictatorship functioned in this way. Even absolutism is consistently precarious and can be maintained only through constant vigilance. It is bound to prompt opposition by its very nature, and hence the informal power brokering of politics. No sovereign can act without regard to informal power and informal constraint. While dictatorships of all sorts lack many of the formal constraints of regimes under the rule of law, they share many of these informal constraints and add to them a number of specific others – pacification of elites, international financial and military support – that fetter power significantly. And, to this extent, it is questionable whether the Schmittian concept of sovereign dictatorship has robust meaning with respect to emergencies. It is a theological fantasy.

Attention to informal as well as formal power and constraint provides a useful tool for critiquing existing institutions as well as for designing new ones. A critique based on the failure to protect *underlying* values is more trenchant. A good set of emergency powers, one that

---

[56] Bruce Ackerman, *Before the Next Attack: Preserving Civil Liberties in an Age of Terrorism.*

would be minimally offensive to liberal principles and maximally effective, will endeavor to shift constraints and enablements in such a way as to meet emergency circumstances effectively while promoting safety and the primary values the rule of law is intended to promote. Because this is continuous with modes of government under normal circumstances, the 'authoritarianism' of emergency powers is not necessarily illiberal, and it is by no means a 'constitutional dictatorship' as long as the emergency provisions are good ones.

Hence, the conception of power and constraint I advocate in this book blurs the distinction between norm and exception. Both normal and emergency circumstances are influenced by similar mechanisms of power and, although the mechanisms of constraint might shift, they are not eliminated, as dichotomous thinking might here advocate. What we might call a 'descriptive' state of exception should not yield an exception from the constraint of power or from normal values and ethics. And this is important. Dichotomous thinking along the lines of norm/exception can be dangerous and we may find ourselves allowing what we should not allow. If we are either with or against our constitutional selves, we risk having to declare against.

The Roman case has provided us with an apt illustration of these elements of emergency. Nonetheless, I do not wish to imply that we can assimilate it directly. It is somewhat puzzling that so many thinkers make use of this Roman institution without drawing attention to what is saliently different in modern government. The reach of modern government and the complex relationships of responsibility between statesmen and their staff make transparency more difficult. Roman political life had a publicity that is all but impossible under contemporary conditions. Moreover, our understanding of political ethics is obviously very different. Nonetheless, the Roman case is useful because the structure of the problem of emergency in constitutional government is the same and because power is a constant in human affairs, even if it flows differently according to the barriers and channels that institutions create.

CONCLUSION

My account of the Roman Dictatorship and its place in the Roman constitution illustrates the fluidity between the rule of law and individual rule, and the range of broader power-related considerations that influence the safety and effectiveness of emergency powers. The Roman Dictatorship has traditionally been employed as an example of a temporary or commissarial absolute rule, but in fact it illustrates this more complex understanding of constraint and enablement better than it does the rule of law dichotomy it is often used to illustrate.

Arguably, most values related to institutions are instrumental.[57] When constitution framers contemplate institutions, tradition and experience – which lend a sense of intrinsic value – play some role, but the *needs* and *ends* of a specific nation form the primary grounds. It is the furthering of equality, liberty, and autonomy through promoting uniformity and predictability that we are really after, not the rule of law itself. Thus, maintaining the rule of law in its 'normal' manifestation would only constitute an ethical-political obligation if it were the only way of furthering these values, which claim I have here tried to call into question.

If there is more to power than the rule of law, then, if the rule of law is not intrinsically valuable, it would follow that there is no *intrinsic* reason to be concerned about a shift away from the rule of law toward more discretionary individual rule. That is to say, the rule of law is not essential; if it is instrumental, and something further can fulfill its instrumental role, such as informal mechanisms of enablement and constraint, then we should be less concerned with a rule of law/individual rule (norm/exception) dichotomy, and more concerned about contemplating effective enablement and constraint in more general terms.

Ultimately, the office holder and the informal constraints that surround the office holder are as important as the office in determining the safety and liberal democratic character of emergency powers. While we may not be willing to go as far as Machiavelli, who claims that "power can easily take a title, but a title cannot give power,"[58] his teaching that the power of an office and that of the person who holds it are not one and the same is worth taking seriously if we wish to make emergencies safer for democracy.

---

[57] It is true that a particular set of institutions may come to be valuable because they are our own, because they are part of our history and in some sense reflect widely shared values. But even this is derivative.

[58] Machiavelli, *Discourses*, 1.34.

6

The Norms of Crisis Government

I have argued that those who justify emergency powers on the basis of exceptionalism free political leaders from moral constraint. This puts citizens at risk. Those who deny any justification for emergency powers by denying exceptions offer an approach that is little safer. They risk the very order that protects and embodies the rights they seek to champion. I have been concerned to show that the norm/exception dichotomy underlying both these perspectives, with which thinkers have long approached the problem of emergency, is wrong conceptually and dangerous in practice. It obscures more than it clarifies. To address this, I have developed in the previous chapters an alternative normative and conceptual framework grounded in the significant continuities between normalcy and emergency.

By rejecting exceptionalism as the framework through which we understand emergency powers, emergency institutions can be brought back within the normative domain. This means that despite the centrality of the rule of law and individual rights to liberal theory, emergency powers can sometimes be justified in a liberal democracy. Because, as I have shown, order and justice are intrinsically connected, and because the values underlying the rule of law can be furthered through a variety of formal and informal means, a liberal democracy can remain liberal democratic even while concentrating power and derogating rights. Emergency powers take on the moral character of the end they serve.

The rigidity of the norm/exception dichotomy obfuscates the range of different kinds of norms that might serve as constraints and hence crisis government easily becomes more dangerous than it need be. But recognizing that norms, both formal and informal, can constrain without strangling emergency power and that rights function constantly alongside order enforcement shows that what differentiates normalcy from emergency is not ontological. Emergency is defined by a cluster of characteristics, none necessarily binary, at the center of which are urgency and scale.

Since restrictions on rights and concentration of power in times of emergency can sometimes be normatively justifiable and correlatively subject to normative constraint, it makes sense to ask what kinds of institutions for crisis government would be normatively optimal. So, having engaged the problem of how emergency powers could *ever* be justifiable, this concluding chapter will raise a number of factors that should bear on making them safer. Emergency institutions must be specific to jurisdictional circumstances, so no single concrete model will be proposed in what follows. Nor will I comment extensively on specific contemporary circumstances, leaving that to the extrapolative interests of my readers. But I will raise a variety of kinds of considerations that should bear on the development of institutions for crisis government. Chief among these is what I will call the 'topographical principle': barriers and channels (disincentives and incentives) of whatever kind are at least as important as borders (formal legal boundaries) in increasing the safety of emergency powers. To show the centrality of this principle, I will explore the long-standing problem of whether crisis action should be embraced within the law (a legal suspension of the law) or banished outside of it. I will argue that formal constraint – law and constitutional provisions – serves a critical purpose, but extra-legal measures are likely a permanent fact of political life. Hence, structuring the incentives that surround both the formal and informal enablement and constraint of emergency government must be our central concern. To this end, I begin by exploring examples of both structures of crisis government, emphasizing the extent to which each is vulnerable and that neither can reasonably be said to constitute a state of exception.

Within the scope of the topographical principle are a number of potential subprinciples drawn from arguments earlier in the book, each of which could inform deliberation and institutional design. Each is in need of empirical and normative development and I will conclude by raising some variables we must take into account.

INSIDE/OUTSIDE

There are many kinds of boundaries at play in the exercise of emergency power. The boundaries of law are the most obvious. They most often constitute those limits the transgression or erasure of which defines exceptionalism in the literature on emergency. But other norms and other boundaries are at work including a variety of conceptions of moral norms and various understandings of legal norms. At this stage, in exploring the variety of approaches to institutional design, it bears keeping in mind the sometimes subtle differences between these types of boundaries. We are interested, in the first instance, in a very specific type of inside/outside relation made clearest through contrast with other forms as we shall now see. Carl Schmitt holds that the idea of emergency is only coherent if it is entirely outside the boundaries of norms as such, both legal and moral. But not all those who would keep emergency power outside of legal boundaries are exceptionalists in this sense. Oren Gross, for instance, holds that while emergency power might best be exercised outside the law to protect the law's integrity, no moral justification can actually erase or trump a violation of law, even though it might justify it. Gross is a legal, but not a moral, exceptionalist. And his legal exceptionalism is not straightforward. There are times when the law should be broken, but the moral quality of the law (as opposed to its legal force) requires that the penalty must then be paid. Posner, by contrast, with his strict utilitarian approach to institutions, argues "that a nonlegal 'law of necessity' . . . would furnish a moral and political justification for acting in contravention of the Constitution [and] may trump constitutional rights in extreme situations"; indeed, "even torture may sometimes be justified in the struggle against terrorism, but it should not be considered *legally* justified."[1] Hence, while the pattern may appear to be the same – "Break the law with a moral justification" – there is an important distinction here. Implicit in Gross's argument is the claim that there are moral considerations inherent in respect for the

---

[1] Richard Posner, *Not a Suicide Pact*, p. 12.

law and inherent in the aims of the law and hence that no general moral excuse can be provided for law breaking, even where law breaking is morally required. For Posner, the utilitarian considerations in question render the law breaker free of moral responsibility. Gross's extra-legal actor must consider his actions worthy of punishment and deeply regrettable. There is shame mixed with heroism. But because Posner has so little concern for the 'sacred' character of the constitution, and because of the extreme nature of his institutional instrumentalism, while the law may still apply, breaking it is fundamentally of as little concern to him as it is to Schmitt. All three of these legal exceptionalists situate their claims for action 'outside' the boundary of law but in different positions with respect to moral boundaries.

Among those advocates of an 'inside' position, perhaps the most sophisticated is David Dyzenhaus, who argues that emergency powers must remain within the purview of the law if the moral integrity of the law is to be respected. A robust conception of the rule of law must be inherent in any coherent understanding of what law is. Mere rule by law is insufficient. Hence, a tacit or explicit moral 'permission' to act outside the law renders the law not-law. At least, not in any meaningful sense. So, on Dyzenhaus's view, not only can we not act outside the law with moral sanction, we cannot *legally* sanction what is not in accordance with a robust moral conception of the rule of law. To avoid black holes and their more dangerous 'gray' cousins, emergency action must remain clearly inside moral and legal boundaries.

What is at stake in the recent debate between Gross and Dyzenhaus along these lines provides a particularly useful starting point for the current inquiry with respect to institutional design for crisis government. What is plausible in each shows both the importance of formal elements of crisis government and their limitations with respect to institutional design. Furthermore, both foreswear moral exceptionalism of the sort that Schmitt or, from a utilitarian standpoint, Posner advocate, a necessary condition for this inquiry, having demonstrated the fundamentally normative character of any acceptable emergency powers. The substance of their respective positions extends back a long way. It structures the contrast between the Roman Dictatorship and the *senatus consultum ultimum*, and between martial law and state of siege. While there is great diversity in the details, the competing models of Dyzenhaus and Gross represent the fundamental forms.

Those who advocate an 'inside' approach to the relevant emergency institutions hold that procedures for crisis government should be outlined in legal or constitutional documents. This increases the formal constraints on emergency action, providing a concrete set of standards against which use of emergency powers can be judged. The Roman Dictatorship – examined at length in Chapter 5 – is a prototype of this formal legal/constitutional structure. The French institution of the state of siege fits this model also. Here, procedures and norms are set out formally in advance, and structure the exercise of emergency power. Contemporary modes of crisis government continue this tradition with a decided trend toward increasing legal specification in the form of extensive legislation, and of international oversight also.

These explicit institutional approaches are not without danger. According to scholars like Gross, Ferejohn, and Pasquino, formal modes of crisis government can infect the normal mode of government, enabling rights limitations to creep beyond what could be justifiable. Furthermore, informal power can, and all too often does, subvert the effectiveness of formal legal constraint. But despite the fact that this form of crisis government is not straightforwardly safe, it has become the dominant form.

The external or extra-legal strategy, which is almost as old as formal, internal emergency measures, purports to solve the problem of contamination by keeping emergency action from legal 'sanctification,' while tacitly supporting illegal action. But, as we saw in Chapter 2 on the origins of exceptionalism, such tacit support *suggests* a two-tier ethics that discourages accountability, while creating few incentives for good behavior. At the same time, there is nothing in this strategy that *establishes* that political officers are in fact above normative considerations, and many theorists of external powers, Gross included, offer models that are strictly reliant on the assumption that political actors would have no such exemption. But, while external emergency powers are not in fact states of exception, they may appear to be such to the political officers themselves, who are *apparently* tacitly excluded from the absoluteness of law. It then remains within the purview of the people or other state mechanisms to attempt to rein them in through informal means. The examples of *senatus consultum ultimum* and martial law will show that under this mode of crisis government, where lines are less clearly drawn, this can be difficult but is far from impossible.

However, insofar as both types represent crisis regimes subject to the constraint of norms of various kinds, they do not represent a contrast between regimes of exception outside the law and regimes governed by law. The distinction between these two modes of crisis government is in that sense overdrawn. This underlines the extent to which a great complexity of kinds of norms interact to enable and constrain emergency powers, as I have argued throughout this book, and as I will now illustrate empirically. They show how, when we set about designing institutions, 'inside' or 'outside' should not be our primary concern. Nonetheless, as we shall see the formal constraint of the law is an important element of the safety of crisis government.

THE INSIDE APPROACH

We now turn to an examination of institutions that illustrate the features characteristic of the 'internal' form of crisis government, showing how they are vulnerable and where they are strong. Most importantly, we see the centrality of informal constraint and informal power, and the ubiquity of nonlegal but still powerful kinds of norms. We begin with the legally sanctioned form of government called state of siege.

State of siege, developed in France in the years immediately following 1791, demonstrates how, while formal mechanisms serve an important purpose, the same mechanisms of informal power that affected the Roman Dictatorship can subvert any structurally similar form of crisis government. It also illustrates how informal constraints in the form of nonlegal norms can help to prevent this.

With the French Declaration of the Rights of Man and the Citizen came the necessity for means of derogation: new constraints on power in the new republic necessitated new forms of enablement. While originally relevant only to places under military attack, the applicability of state of siege continually broadened and contracted with the chaotic conditions following the revolution. The law was finally cemented in a decree of 1848. In response to worker unrest and the general chaos of the new republic, General Louis Eugène Cavaignac was given dictatorial powers.[2] Placing Paris under a state of siege, Cavaignac bombarded barricades, engaged in summary executions, and banished citizens to the new colony of Algeria, which he himself had recently conquered. The 'June Days' uprising was thus stamped out, and moderate republicanism was temporarily restored. These abuses led to the inclusion in the 1848 constitution of Article 106 enabling a state of siege that would function according to specifications prescribed by law. Laws were duly drawn up in 1849 and then revised to fit more modern administrative needs in 1878. These legal provisions carefully specified the conditions under which a state of siege might be declared, who could declare it, and who must concur. They also specified how long the state of siege might remain in effect and the specific powers that the military might assume. The emergency powers that a state of siege provided to the government included vesting police powers in the military and restrictions on privacy rights. The military was empowered to search houses, to evacuate those in an area under threat who did not reside there, to confiscate weapons, to restrict rights to freedom of speech and assembly, and to censor the press. Finally, a state of siege meant certain crimes could be tried before a military rather than a civilian court.

Both the 1848 and the 1878 laws state specifically that citizens maintain their constitutional rights during a state of siege. And the 1878 law carefully restricted its application to times of *immediate* threat "resulting from a foreign war or an armed insurrection."[3] Responsibility for such declarations was transferred to the legislature or, if the legislature was not sitting, a president's declaration was subject to later ratification or nullification. Increasing specification meant, for the most part, increasingly formal safeguards and constraints.

In the French legislation, we know exactly who may proclaim a state of siege and under exactly what kinds of circumstances. We also know

---

[2] It is interesting to note how closely Cavaignac's fascinating career mirrors that of the Roman dictators. His military achievements in conquering Algeria led to prestigious public posts, culminating in his appointment as dictator. After his success as dictator, he engineered sweeping popular constitutional reforms aimed at further democratizing the republic and alleviating the poverty of the urban unemployed through state-sponsored work programs. This led him to a run for president, but he was soundly defeated by Louis Napoleon, to whom, upon his assumption of the title of Emperor, Cavaignac refused to swear an oath.

[3] Quoted in Charles Fairman, *The Law of Martial Rule*, p. 68. My translation.

exactly which rights may be derogated, and even the procedures for appealing such derogations. Fairman points out that "a citizen might sue in an administrative tribunal to have an arête ... annulled for *excès de pouvoir*. Or he might wait until he was proceeded against in the ordinary courts, and then challenge the arête as *ultra vires*."[4] Norms are evident in the formal constraints displayed in the justiciability of tribunal decisions, and in the informal constraints evident in the to and fro of legal infringements on executive discretion. Clearly, the moral aspects of state of siege were the subject of deliberation and debate.[5] The French state of siege is no state of exception.

Nonetheless, these formal provisions, like all laws, emergency-related or otherwise, are operationalized selectively and in accordance with political conditions. Just because a law is written does not mean that it will necessarily be enforced, or enforced as intended, even if formal legal provisions do help. Legal provisions provide a public set of standards for deliberation and debate, and this can make accountability, if not certain, then at least less difficult, because these standards are clear to all.

---

[4] Quoted in Charles Fairman, *The Law of Martial Rule*, p. 68. My translation.
[5] Joseph Minattur has argued that the reason French state of siege contains so many explicit limitations while British martial law does not is that France was responding to past executive abuses. However, if we look at the history of British emergency action, this argument looks weak. Emergency powers in Britain were a constant subject of contention between the Crown and parliament, so much so, that the emergency Ship Money measure of Charles I is sometimes cited as the scandal that raised the axe above his head. Questions of emergency prerogative, and Stuart abuses of martial law were very near the center of Britain's seventeenth century constitutional crises. Hence, to claim that France's bad experiences with emergency government directly caused its careful specification of emergency powers in the 1878 legislation seems implausible. Furthermore, if this argument were sound, we would expect colonial regimes that had suffered under British martial law to dispense with this mode of government, or at least to rein it in yet further. On the contrary, post-colonial regimes on the whole adopted those versions of British emergency powers that were contemporary when their constitutions were first drawn up. Minattur's argument for the source of the different levels of specification holds little weight. See Minattur, *Martial Law in India, Pakistan, and Ceylon*, p. 13. One might conject that the differences in common and civil law traditions are more likely to account for the differences between the French and British systems of emergency government prior to World War I. The British system of common law involves grouping together cases with like empirical circumstances, while the civil law tradition involves determining and then applying the right abstract principle, such that like cases need not be treated alike. Britain had available to it a common law full of principles restricting the use of martial law. These principles functioned as a means of constraint. But for those employing civil law, such principles could not be relied upon unless they were made positive.

While there is evidence that extra-legal "emergency" action continues in secret in many democratic regimes, the 1878 state of siege provisions mark the beginning of a worldwide shift toward the formal codification of crisis government and positive legal constraints on emergency power. This has taken a number of forms, constitutional and legal, domestic and international, and has combined a number of elements. France's state of siege, for instance, has been incorporated into the constitutions of a large number of former French colonial possessions, as well as the constitutions of many Latin American and African countries where these provisions have been subject to frequent abuse. This shows the extent to which informal considerations still figure despite clear formal constraints.[6]

One key feature of contemporary emergency powers that serves as a potential means of offsetting this danger has been to tie both power concentration and rights derogations procedures to the seriousness of the situation. Because lesser powers are available for less serious situations, it places a greater burden on political leaders to match their actions to the seriousness of the situation. Canada's legislative emergency powers framework, for example, provides specific provisions for different kinds of scenarios with regard to rights derogations. The provisions vary in weight from public welfare emergencies to war emergencies. The former are natural or health-related disasters such as droughts, floods, or epidemics, and they warrant rights derogations that include restrictions on movement, evacuation, and so on.[7] If security is seriously and immediately threatened a public order emergency may be declared, which enables "limitations on free assembly, travel, and the free use of property," and provides for forced labor.[8] An international emergency will mean the declaration process is streamlined and the range of derogable rights widened: removal of nonresident aliens for security purposes, control of industry, home searches[9] when there is "an emergency involving Canada and one or more other countries that arises from acts of intimidation or coercion or the real or imminent use of serious force or violence and that is so serious as to

---

[6] See, for example, John Hatchard, *Individual Freedoms and State Security in the African Context.*

[7] *Emergencies Act* (Canada 1985), Art. 8(1).

[8] *Emergencies Act* (Canada 1985), Art. 19(1).

[9] *Emergencies Act* (Canada 1985), Art. 30(1).

be a national emergency."[10] And finally a war emergency can be declared when armed conflict is imminent or immediate, and goes yet further. This kind of tiered legislation provides a safety buffer against abuses of rights not strictly necessitated by the circumstances. Germany's constitution delivers a further example, where Article 115 sets out different checks and balances tailored to the degree of urgency.[11]

Specification not only formally enables action in a crisis and informally constrains by rhetorical means, it can also add new means of formal constraint. Spain, for example, employs a combination of constitutional and legislative provisions that serve to criminalize abuse of emergency powers. The Spanish constitution (1978) states that the content of emergency provisions should be laid out in legislation. But Article 55, section 2.2, sets down that "The unwarranted or abusive utilization of the powers recognized in said organic law will result in criminal responsibility as a violation of the rights and liberties recognized by the law." Making liability for abuse of emergency powers foundational, while leaving the details to legislators, provides a certain flexibility even though its scope is bound within carefully specified and at least theoretically enforceable norms.

In addition, many newer constitutions contain specific limitations borrowed almost verbatim from the chief document in international law pertaining to emergency powers, the International Covenant on Civil and Political Rights (ICCPR). Article 4 of the ICCPR explicitly allows for derogations to *some* of the rights contained elsewhere in that document for the purpose of bounding emergency powers within a human rights framework. This article sets out a number of rights that can *never* be derogated, and thereby sets definite limits and a clear definition of abuse. It was the decision, however contentious, of the international community that safety was on the side of openness and specificity about emergencies.

Not everyone shares this opinion. For one, there is empirical evidence that signing on to the ICCPR is no guarantee that political leaders will actually be governed by its articles. Zambia, for example, declared a state of emergency in 1993 that fairly clearly violated the requirements of the

---

[10] *Emergencies Act* (Canada 1985), Art. 27.
[11] *German Basic Law*, Chapter Xa: State of Defense.

convention, despite the fact that Zambia is a signatory.[12] A lack of informal pressure from the international community, coupled with domestic support, sometimes means political leaders face much stronger incentives to violate than to respect the law and international agreements with respect to emergency. We can see this in the cases of Egypt (for most of the twentieth century) and India (1975–77) as well. Both had sophisticated legal and constitutional provisions governing emergencies, but political considerations made these formal constraints far less effective. Law is not enough.

Recent scholarship has emphasized other potential dangers of formally enabling crisis government. Gross's "extra-legal measures" model of emergency powers, for example, grows from a concern that crisis can, and often does, continue for decades and decades such that it becomes the norm. This blurs the distinction between descriptive normalcy and descriptive states of exception. If emergency powers are legally sanctioned, this leaves open the possibility that serious emergency action could continue indefinitely, while failing to draw public notice or concern. Gross has argued that "Allowing the constitution to prescribe its own suspension confers a false sense of legality and legitimacy on these exceptional measures and facilitates the breaking down of the demarcation lines between normalcy and emergency."[13] On this view, a set of legally mandated emergency powers courts disaster and, even with such powers, there may be extreme cases, such as the temptation to torture, that we would wish never to flirt with legality. In their article "The Law of Exception: a Typology of Emergency Powers," Ferejohn and Pasquino argue that differentiating normalcy and exception is critical for safety.[14] For Ferejohn and Pasquino, as for Gross, differentiating ontologically between emergency and normal regimes keeps rights derogations from creeping into those areas of political life where they should not be.

But in codifying the would-be exception, contemporary emergency provisions *do* surround emergency with formal norms. Positive rules enmeshed with principles – some continuous and some specific to

---

[12] John Hatchard, "States of Siege/Emergency in Africa."
[13] Oren Gross, "Providing for the Unexpected: Constitutional Emergency Provisions," p. 27.
[14] Ferejohn and Pasquino, "The Law of Exception: A Typology of Emergency Powers," p. 221.

emergency – can combine with an elaborate web of means of accountability: through the courts, through elections, through tribunal oversight, and so on. Informal constraints include the institutional tradition, the higher republican existential norms related to the preservation of the state in a functional form, and the public reputation of those who make use of emergency powers. While these norms are not always enforced, they are at least delineated. When political officers abuse emergency power, we can then point to the standard they failed to meet, to what would count as *use* rather than abuse.

Understanding those institutions that keep emergency powers within the law through enablement and constraint provides a more illuminating conceptual framework. It demonstrates that emergencies are not states of exception, and that the formal legal constraints associated with an internal style of crisis government do not provide a foolproof means to safety.

THE OUTSIDE APPROACH

So much less foolproof is maintaining a 'safe' distance from emergency measures by keeping them at arm's length, beyond the law, as we shall now see from these examples of modes of governing in a crisis that employ powers external to formal, written law.

The prototype of this constitutional structure was the so-called *senatus consultum ultimum*. Dictatorship, as a standing institution of Roman republican government, was not Rome's only emergency institution. When the military conditions that had given rise to the need for that institution changed, the dictatorship no longer provided an effective institutional means of addressing emergencies. The Romans developed the *senatus consultum ultimum* as an alternative. In effect, the senate instructed a consul that Rome was under serious threat, and that he should take any measures necessary to address it. Beyond this, the consul was on his own. The *senatus consultum ultimum* had no pseudo-constitutional character. There was no standing provision of formal enablement, nor were there formal rules of constraint specific to this form of crisis government. Hence, this institution can be understood as a proto-extra-legal measure.

Nonetheless, in other ways, a consul acting under a *consultum ultimum* worked under greater restrictions than had dictators in the earlier periods, insofar as the rights of the plebeians had by this time become increasingly formal. The earliest dictators did not have to contend with the *provocatio ad populum* – the right of the people to decide on capital cases – but the consuls did. Under a *consultum ultimum*, a consul could violate this right if he thought it was strictly necessary to achieve his aim, but should he step even a little beyond the bounds of what the people understood as strict necessity, he could expect to be held to account. Here, flexibility trumped safety before the fact with a variety of principles as well as rules governing the consuls' actions. Safety came in the form of an informal threat made credible by the knowledge that it was often enforced. Accountability after the fact was an ever-present possibility.

For example, consider the famous incidents of Opimius and Cicero. In 121 B.C., Gaius Gracchus, a populist tribune, seized control of the Aventine Hill following the assassination of an official by some of his supporters. In response, the senate issued the then consul, Opimius, a *senatus consultum ultimum*. Having executed certain citizens under its authority, he was charged with a violation of Roman due process. He was acquitted. Some sixty years later, Cicero, consul in 63 B.C., executed some Catilinarian conspirators without a trial. He, like Opimius, was charged, and Cicero, unlike Opimius, was found guilty. Opimius did what was necessary in the opinion of Rome's citizens, but Cicero went beyond that.

The *senatus consultum ultimum* relies on a consul's judgment and flexibility coupled with accountability after the fact. It is constituted by a delicate balance of unusual enablement and new forms of (mostly informal) constraint. It is highly probable that politics, the informal flow of power and constraint, had much to do with the differing fates of Cicero and Opimius. But norms as such are not suspended. There is no state of exception. Formal mechanisms were available but were tacitly suspended. Politics intervenes to determine whether or not the suspension is maintained. Informal power and informal constraint are still central.

This structure's lack of formal legal constraint, coupled with standing principles and *post facto* accountability in the *senatus consultum ultimum*, is mirrored with some exactness in the martial law regimes of pre-1914 Britain and its colonies. Here too measures are somewhat extra-legal, but a multiplicity of norms continues to function and to be enforced in accordance with informal constraints. As with the *senatus consultum ultimum*, these constraints are primarily political.

Of the variety of senses in which the term 'martial law' has been used,[15] the one with which we are concerned is the one that came into currency in England after the Petition of Right (1628). It is the enforcement of discipline within the military and the control of civilian populations in times of war. With a declaration of martial law, principle and custom enable tighter control of civilian populations and more efficient execution of domestic military aims. As in the Roman case, the impetus for the development of martial law in Great Britain was the existence of a constitutional structure[16] with divided powers and individual rights.[17] And, as in the Roman case, the chief bone of contention as martial law developed concerned a balance between regulations bounding a statesman's behavior before the fact and accountability to principles after the fact.

The common law of England and the constitution of the United States have always provided certain post-facto remedies, and these remedies refer to a variety of kinds of norms, despite the fact that martial law might look like what Sir Matthew Hale in his *History of the Common Law of England* describes as lawlessness.[18] The freedom martial law bestows is not without constraint. Indeed, courts have historically enforced limits on the free imposition of martial law, if not immediately, then eventually. Martial law has affinities with the defense of necessity and with self-defense,[19] both recognized in the common law. While it would not be correct to claim that one is derived

---

[15] Good overviews of the legislative history of martial law in Great Britain are W. S. Holdsworth, "Martial Law Historically Considered"; Fairman, *The Law of Martial Rule*; G. G. Phillimore, "Martial Law in Rebellion."

[16] Though, of course, they have no *formal* constitution.

[17] Of course, Roman citizens did not have rights in the sense that we use the term, but they had morally equivalent entitlements with respect to relations with those who governed them.

[18] Sir Matthew Hale has said "Touching the business of martial law, these things are to be observed, viz.: . . . That in truth and reality it is not a law, but something indulged rather than allowed as a law; the necessity of government, order, and discipline in an army, is that only which can give those laws a countenance: *quod enim necessitas cogit defendit.*" *The History of the Common Law of England*, p. 54.

[19] Sir James Fitzjames Stephens argues that martial law is "the common law right of the Crown and its representatives to repel force by force in the case of invasion or insurrection, and to act against rebels as it might against invaders." *A History of the Criminal Law of England*, vol. 1, p. 208. Dicey, in *Introduction to the Study of the Law of the Constitution*, concurs, calling martial law "the power of the government or of loyal citizens to maintain public order, at whatever cost of blood or property may be necessary," p. 286.

from the other, they trace their source to the same principle. As with an individual who might offer those defenses for a crime, it has traditionally been the courts that after the fact have held to account the wielders of martial law. Just as individual judgment determines how much force to use in self-defense, with hope that a judge or jury will concur, so a statesman who acts through a declaration of martial law must face the judgment of parliament and of citizens at large whether in court or at the polls.

Both criminal and civil remedies have been available to citizens whose rights have been abused without justification. Norms of various important kinds continue in effect. The examples of Hawai'i (1941–44) and Jamaica (1865) provide ample illustration.

Harry and Jane Scheiber have written an extensive account of the political and legal wrangling surrounding the Hawai'an case.[20] It shows very clearly both the dangers and the possibilities inherent in post facto justification. For three years following the 1941 attack on Pearl Harbor, Hawai'ians lived under a strict martial law regime designed to prevent further attacks, invasion, and treason. Many of the measures enforced under martial law could not have been enforced under normal legal conditions. A nightly blackout meant anyone caught lighting a cigarette after dark or anyone whose radio dial glowed too close to the window could be arrested and fined or imprisoned. The blackout was intended to prevent targeted bombings. Measures aimed at making saboteurs and infiltrators easier to spot included the requirement that Hawai'ians over the age of six carry identification and a ban on possessing more than $200 in cash. In an effort to prevent espionage, censorship was sweeping. Authorities read mail leaving the islands and all phone conversations had to be conducted in English so that the military could listen in. Most tragically, the remedy of habeas corpus was suspended and 1,141 of the 150,000 Japanese-Americans in Hawai'i were taken into custody, with 980 men and women remaining under lock and key until the end of the war.[21] Civil cases were tried by military tribunal, often without counsel, without the option of a jury,

---

[20] See Harry N. Scheiber and Jane L. Scheiber, "Bayonets in Paradise: A Half-Century Retrospect on Martial Law in Hawai'i, 1941–1946."

[21] A particularly interesting account of the jurisprudence of habeas corpus, albeit primarily focused on the United Kingdom, is R. J. Sharpe, *The Law of Habeas Corpus*.

and with little or no possibility of an appeal. This included cases that had no conceivable connection to the military situation.

These draconian measures, necessary or otherwise, were clearly unconstitutional. It is for this very reason that martial law was declared. For, if the government of Hawai'i had wished to undertake measures that were already legal martial law might not have been required.[22] Historically there have been no formal rules governing the day-to-day exercise of a regime of martial law; there is no codified legal framework. While martial law is in force, there is enormous freedom of scope for maintaining order and control. But here, as with the *senatus consultum ultimum*, the situation is not straightforward. In Hawai'i, civil liberties groups and members of the civil government were hard at work fighting the martial law regime almost as soon as it was instituted.[23] They met with equally vociferous opposition. Eventually, after a number of strategic machinations and press and political interventions on both sides, the opponents of martial law succeeded, in 1944, in convincing a federal judge to call the whole thing off. When the military authorities ignored the judge, President Roosevelt intervened personally. After the war, a number of citizens who had suffered under the martial law regime sought and won legal redress. Of course this is very far from ideal and is not intended to minimize the enormous suffering generated by this episode in history, some of which was certainly avoidable. My point is not that all was well in Hawai'i. Rather, this episode illustrates aspects of the legal and political complexity of martial law that tell against a characterization as a state of exception from law. Were this a true state of exception, this kind of accountability and the very notion of legal redress would be incoherent. Even measures that are not formally enabled by law can still be subject to normative and even legal redress if the political situation supports it.

---

[22] An exception would be a situation in which a political leader declares an emergency for the purpose of ensuring that citizens are aware of the seriousness of the situation, or, as in both Canada and the United States, with the intent to obtain federal emergency funding, which might be available only when an emergency has actually been declared.

[23] Some of the figures involved in the political and legal wrangling during this period took their battle to the law reviews and the press. See, for instance, Garner Anthony, "Martial Law, Military Government and the Writ of Habeas Corpus in Hawaii."

As with the *senatus consultum ultimum,* an extra-legal declaration and accountability after the fact could lead to trouble. Political considerations loom larger with this mode and the incentive structures do not necessarily run in a desirable direction. Much engineering of informal constraints would be necessary, and even then this is a dangerous set-up.

This is made even clearer by the case of Jamaica in 1865. Throughout the nineteenth century, martial law was an important tool of colonial and domestic military administration for both Great Britain and the United States. Britain employed martial law in an effort to control uprisings in Demerara (1832), Canada (1848), Jamaica (1865), and elsewhere.[24] A colonial governor who declared martial law had to expect, under British jurisprudence, that his actions would be regarded as technically criminal. This is confirmed both by the fact that the British parliament occasionally passed an indemnity act after a period of martial law, and by the fact that some governors were actually brought to court. The most famous such case followed the Jamaican uprising of 1865. Governor Eyre, by all accounts a generally mild-mannered man and a decent administrator, declared martial law in parts of Jamaica in response to a massacre purportedly meant to signal the start of a rebellion. While he was careful to confine his declaration to certain areas, his soldiers went on a murderous rampage, burning houses, executing people without so much as a superior's command, never mind a trial, and generally terrorizing local people. Worse still, he arranged for the arrest of a political opponent, George Gordon, and for his transportation from Kingston, which was not under martial law, to an area that was. There, Gordon was tried and hanged by Judge Advocates General. The Governor Eyre case was a *cause célèbre* and a matter of political importance. In Britain, a number of notable intellectuals and politicians, including, for example, John Stuart Mill, intervened. Finally, for his abuse of martial power Eyre and two of his officers,

[24] Fairman says that "in the British Empire 'martial law' followed by an act of indemnity has been a device whereby servile and native uprisings have been stamped out, often with more celerity than decorum." *The Law of Martial Rule,* p. 26. For an illustrative account of British colonial use of martial law, please see Minattur, *Martial Law in India, Pakistan, and Ceylon.* See also the nineteenth-century account in W. F. Finalson, *Review of the Authorities as the Repression of Riot or Rebellion with Special Reference to Criminal or Civil Liability;* and for an excellent, more contemporary discussion of colonial emergency jurisprudence, see Nasser Hussain, *The Jurisprudence of Emergency.*

Nelson and Brand, were brought before a Grand Jury in England on charges of murder. The Grand Jury found that Eyre had acted "honestly" but nonetheless insisted that the law should provide more explicit and formal guidance on the principles governing martial law. Martial law was justified according to a principle of the common law holding "that life may be protected and crime prevented by the immediate application of any amount of force which, under the circumstances, may be necessary."[25]

Martial law, much like the *senatus consultum ultimum*, begins with a declaration that a crisis is in progress, that something must be done to 'save the republic,' governed by the norm that whatever *is* done must be just enough and no more than is strictly necessary to resolve the situation. Thereafter, informal constraints, subject as they are to political machinations, take over. A similar perspective has most recently been championed by Oren Gross. Gross proposes that in a crisis, a statesman or administrator should choose to break the law: he or she is not empowered by law to act, but rather ought to act decisively against the law. The authority in so doing is not legal, but somehow moral. Thereafter, officials are (morally) obliged to disclose their actions and throw themselves on the mercy of the public. Whether or not such behavior is excusable is then judged on a case-by-case basis. No one slips under the radar because emergency action is legal and normalized, and, because such extra-legal action is so extreme and so public, it reduces the chances that 'bad' behavior will come to characterize the legal order. It remains illegal – with attendant consequences – if the public cannot be convinced of its necessity. Because indemnification of some kind is not guaranteed, Gross thinks this arrangement will act as a deterrent.

Even on Gross's "voluntary" model, the presence of normative oversight, both moral oversight and to an extent legal oversight, shows that this style of crisis government is not intended as and does not strictly function as a state of exception. And Gross is correct that this structure avoids some of the dangers of a legal model. Nonetheless, it is not as safe as it could be. Gross's model, like the *senatus consultum ultimum* and martial law, depends heavily on incentives for good behavior, and great care must be taken in such a system with respect to how these are

[25] Cited in Holdsworth, "Martial Law Historically Considered," p. 122.

constructed. Incentives naturally run in the other direction, because crisis government is often secret,[26] and because crisis conditions and the correlative fear lead citizens to a more indulgent attitude toward government action. We have seen that these factors certainly do not prevent oversight, but they do not encourage it either.

Partly because of these dangers, it is now highly unusual for a state to lack any form of legislative or constitutional emergency power. Formal constraints in one form or another govern states of emergency over much of the world. No rigorous empirical study has, to my knowledge, been conducted to determine which mode of crisis government, in the final analysis, is safest under which conditions. But from this discussion two things become demonstrably, empirically clear. First, states of emergency are clearly not states of exception in practice. A wide range of normative constraints can be brought into play in crisis conditions and hence any 'moment of exception' is a normative choice, not an existential fact. This is to say that if a particular political officer chooses to break the law or subvert a formal constraint, that transgression may instance a moment of freedom, but the freedom is of the same kind as the freedom of anyone who breaks the law. A person who murders may, in that split second, exempt him or herself from the 'government of the law' just as well. But the sovereignty of this form of transgression makes the transgressor sovereign over a kingdom of one, and that sovereignty lasts no longer than the very moment of transgression.

Second, we can see that what is most salient with respect to these different approaches is not the 'external' or 'internal' aspect so much as the effectiveness of different forms of constraint or enablement more generally. This difference is parallel to the difference between a political map, which emphasizes borders and jurisdictions, and a topographic map, which shows the features of a landscape, the physical barriers and the pathways and riverbeds between them. The physical features of a landscape can be understood to affect each other: mountains channel the flow of rivers but rivers erode their banks. The same can be said with respect to politics, as the new institutionalists demonstrate. The formal elements of law, the legal enablements, and the legal constraints

---

[26] Simon Chesterman, "Deny Everything: Intelligence Activities and the Rule of Law in Times of Crisis."

of institutions channel the flow of power, but political agency structures and consistently remolds institutions. The fluid aspects of power shape the formal aspects over time, and sometimes find their way over or around the barriers that formal power erects.[27]

Hence, we come to what I am calling the topographical principle for the design of safer emergency powers. We must take account of not only formal, but also informal mechanisms of enablement and constraint, emphasizing the importance of informal powers specific to emergency. Beginning from an assumption of normlessness prevents fruitful engagement with the complex normative and institutional possibilities of emergency powers. We cease to see them, or to recognize them for what they are, and this effectively prevents constructive engagement with this pressing institutional and normative problem.

While no set of emergency powers can avoid the many difficulties this chapter raises, good institutions should set up formal, public criteria for the sound use of emergency powers and should at a minimum invoke an automatic mechanism for their enforcement. Such criteria would be both normative and procedural. Normative principles might include, for example, the 'necessity principle': whenever a political leader makes a claim of necessity, we should demand that it be accompanied by a clear chain of reasons leading from the action undertaken to the result deemed necessary. This contributes to safety because, to the extent that alternatives appear in the course of this chain of reasons, we can evaluate each, and hence determine the least invasive course of action.

Normative principles might also include the 'urgency and scale principle': insofar as the core differences between preservation of order in emergency and in nonemergency are urgency and scale, any use of emergency powers should address these two factors specifically. Shifts in institutional and moral norms should be directly related to empirical differences in emergency circumstances.

While no mechanism based on these principles would be fail-safe, these would contribute to the balance of incentives toward good behavior. In order to facilitate accountability, these principles could be incorporated into legislation and widely publicized whenever an emergency is

---

[27] I discuss this in greater detail in my "Topography of Emergency Power," in Ramraj (ed.), *Emergencies and the Limits of Legality*, pp. 156–71.

declared. Moreover, where possible, the reasons for the emergency declaration and for each power invoked under its authority should be set out in advance of any emergency action, and it is according to these reasons and these criteria that political leaders will be held to account. This will facilitate public deliberation and evaluation, particularly after the fact.

Once public criteria have been set up, some means of enforcing them must also come into play. Because deliberation may be cut short in an emergency, and because secrecy or surprise might be useful in certain cases, good emergency powers should incorporate an automatic mechanism of after-the-fact accountability. The promise of accountability according to clear criteria is an important element of constraint on concentrated power, but the test in such a case should not be whether a political leader was in fact justified but rather whether a reasonable person would have felt justified in declaring a state of emergency. For, we do not wish to make the burdens of office unbearable. Citizens will inevitably have a difficult time gauging how things looked to their leader in the heat of the moment and so accountability on the basis of deliberation after the fact will not necessarily yield the same conclusion based on the same information. It may be very difficult to reconstruct the situation as it was. Absent a political leader who is also an extraordinary storyteller, it would be enormously difficult to *show* how things looked at the time, and because of the elements of judgment and moral complexity, it is nearly impossible to *tell*.[28]

Moreover, citizens are likely to defend their rights more vigorously once a danger has passed, and not every citizen will be affected in the same way by an emergency. Hence, how different interest groups manage the political elements of accountability will have a significant effect on outcomes regardless of formal constraints. All these factors would have to be taken into consideration in designing means of accountability with the end of providing effective informal constraint. And the designers of emergency institutions will also have to take care to minimize the temptation for political opponents to abuse sanctions for ill-applied emergency powers when power changes hands.

---

[28] Stuart Hampshire suggests that, while it is almost as difficult to reconstruct moral reasoning as it is to reconstruct our choice of diction, reconstruction is important to judging after the fact, because of the likelihood, in moral cases, of emotions getting in the way. Hampshire (ed.), *Public and Private Morality*, p. 29.

These nascent principles for safety stem from the arguments in this book. We saw the centrality of informal constraint and enablement in Chapter 5, which strongly suggests the topographical principle. The importance of principles dealing with urgency and scale and the moral sense of necessity was explored in Chapter 4. And the essential character of accountability emerged from our discussions of exceptionalism in Chapter 2.

But the principles that have emerged from my arguments are indeed only nascent. In order to develop concrete suggestions for institutions specific to particular jurisdictions, an enormous amount of further systematic empirical research is necessary. Such research must take into account the critical nature of context. The whole political context is relevant, not just the emergency itself. How do a particular jurisdiction's everyday institutions make an emergency more or less likely? How might political leaders be held accountable for preventable emergencies in addition to emergency powers abuses?

Because, as I have argued, only the most moral means are justified in fulfilling a moral duty, it is arguably a duty in itself, a normative matter, to take up this empirical work. To make emergencies safer we need a better understanding of how they unfold in practice. We know very little about the empirical correlates of different forms of emergency powers: about which kinds of existing institutional structures and which kinds of political conditions work best with which emergency institutions. It would be well worth finding out.[29]

Among those variables that an empirical inquiry would have to take into account would be federal structure, existence and functions of a constitutional court, means of public finance, electoral system, and the conception of rights in a particular state's political tradition. Because the question of federalism is particularly important and because the question of a rights tradition is particularly interesting, I will elaborate just these two.

Federalism touches on and complicates nearly every aspect of emergency. For example, central government is often constitutionally empowered to force a lesser jurisdiction to abide by the constitution.

---

[29] Unfortunately, the relative rarity of serious emergencies and the recent vintage of most sets of emergency powers might mean that data would be too scarce to enable rigorous empirical testing to be conducted.

Both Weimar in the 1920s and 1930s and India in 1975, two of the most famous cases of emergency powers, involved this kind of inter-jurisdictional wrangling. And Americans will remember how the President of the United States called out the National Guard to enforce the end of school segregation in the southern states. Furthermore, federal funding arrangements can affect the declaration of states of emergency. In the United States, historically, access to funds for disaster relief through the Federal Emergency Management Agency (FEMA) only becomes possible when a state declares an emergency. Similarly, in Canada, federal funds and other aid, such as the provision of army labor, are made available only when an emergency is declared by a province or municipality. The incentives thus provided should be examined and alternatives sought. Finally, a federal structure like that of the European Union with its Court of Human Rights might serve as an effective constraint both for informal political reasons and through formal mechanisms of accountability. Federalism matters in emergencies.

In teasing out and operationalizing principles for emergency government, it might also be worth paying heed to differences in cultural and historical understandings of rights. For example, it is a striking fact that many of Britain's former colonial possessions have constitutions that situate emergency powers directly after the rights catalogue, as though derogations were an inherent part of rights. Other states situate their emergency powers in a separate section or scatter them among the specific provisions they derogate. Differences in the placement of derogation provisions might reflect differences in emphasis. Those states that outline emergency powers along with rights presumably have a weaker conception of the status of rights. In the same breath, they are granted and qualified. Perhaps they never quite had the absoluteness, self-evidence, and naturalness of the rights of the French or the Americans in the first place.

Chapter III of the Constitution of the Bahamas (1973), for example, provides a catalogue of rights. But Article 29 of the very same chapter provides that only a handful of rights (drawn from the ICCPR) are nonderogable. Only these few might be allowed to interfere with effective emergency government. Similarly, the Canadian Charter of Rights and Freedoms (1982) begins with a statement about the potential for derogation, not just in emergency circumstances but always. And

Section 91 of the Constitution of Canada (1867) states that, "It shall be lawful for the Queen, by and with the Advice and Consent of the Senate and House of Commons, to make Laws for the Peace, Order, and good Government of Canada." This is explicitly set out as the primary and most significant purpose of government. In these states, the constitutions themselves emphasize a certain relationship between order and the prerogatives of the state itself, between rights and the limitations imposed by duties. Emergency circumstances constitute just one more rights limitation.[30] Hence, attention to the colonial origins of a constitution is also worthwhile in empirical inquiry into emergency government.

Perhaps, over the course of time, the culture of rights that the United Nations rights documents have engendered will continue to bring about a shift in the rights philosophies of these countries toward the original French and American models. And perhaps, as Kim Lane Scheppele has argued, those states with a long history of fundamental rights will lag in justice behind those with a new commitment to rights regimes.[31] When this is achieved, what will be lost is the insight that rights, unlike the moral information underlying them, are not like the laws of physics: immutable and absolute. What will be gained is the insight that, because of the moral information rights carry, those who violate rights dirty their hands.

CONCLUSION

Political leaders must be held accountable when they dirty their hands, something exceptionalism does not allow. But this statement marks the beginning, not the end, of an inquiry because the complex relationship between representatives, citizens, and states is philosophically opaque. With respect to emergency powers, further inquiry is warranted here as

[30] For interesting discussions of the concept of rights limitations in the Canadian context, see Janet L. Hiebert, *Limiting Rights*; Kenneth Fogarty, *Equality Rights and Their Limitation in the Charter*.

[31] Scheppele has recently argued, in the manuscript for a book to be called *The International State of Emergency* (http://digitalcommons.law.umaryland.edu/schmooze_papers/49), that, in fact, the 'founding' rights cultures, such as that of the United States, have grown less reliable with respect to upholding rights in times of challenge than those like Canada that have recently actively and consciously embraced a rights culture.

well. If, as I have argued, political leaders are morally compelled to do wrong while rights remain in force, they are morally compelled to dirty their hands. Michael Walzer, in his classic article on the subject, posed the dilemma as follows: "sometimes it is right to try to succeed, and then it must also be right to get one's hands dirty. But one's hands get dirty from doing what it is wrong to do. And how can it be wrong to do what is right? Or, how can we get our hands dirty by doing what we ought to do?"[32] We might add: how can we hold a leader accountable for what he or she is morally obliged to do? The arguments of this book have posed an answer to one part of this question that rests on the fundamentally political nature of the problem. Because of the specifically political context of emergency, we have what might best be termed a collective problem of dirty hands that remains to be illuminated.

In the last century, the problem of dirty hands caught the attention of a number of political thinkers, particularly at times when such choices came forcefully to light: in Weimar Germany, during World War II in Europe and America, and during the Vietnam War.[33] Yet, with the exception of Sartre and Weber, the literature that arose out of each of these periods does not confront the ethical character of the state itself and its importance to the moral nature of emergency political action. They do not differentiate between decisions that are morally tragic, which those in positions of authority are simply more likely to confront, and those situations that are essentially political. While many of the writers are quick to point out that it is not only politicians who face dirty-handed choices, those choices politicians face are importantly ethically different. Sartre has illustrated this well. A critical element in the action of his play *Les mains sales* is that the revolutionary character, Hoederer, is trying to found a political community. It is not simply that he is trying to bring about some good, or avoid some worse evil. The fact that the good he is trying to bring about is a political community is importantly relevant because he sees a certain kind of ethics made possible within such a political community.[34] It is not

---

[32] Michael Walzer, "Political Action and the Problem of Dirty Hands," p. 164.

[33] See, for instance, Max Weber, "Politics as a Vocation"; Jean-Paul Sartre, *Les mains sales*; Stanley I. Benn, "Private and Public Morality: Clean Living and Dirty Hands"; Stuart Hampshire (ed.), *Public and Private Morality*; Martin Hollis, "Dirty Hands"; Paul Rynard and David Shugarman (eds.), *Cruelty and Deception*.

[34] Sartre, *Les mains sales*, V.iii.

simply that good things will come of its founding, generally speaking, but that there will be new kinds of good things. In other words, Hoederer refers to an existential ethics.

But dirty hands arguments that ignore the political element of the problem are impoverished in more than an explanatory sense. In Chapter 1, I suggested that we might move between the justice of emergency institutions and the justice of emergency action because the agency of our political leaders, especially at such times, is itself a political institution. In removing the political element, those who write on the subject of dirty hands confront the problem of moral tragedy (of which emergency powers are certainly one instance) as though an executive acts qua simple moral agent. "Why," asks Stanley Benn, "should reasons of expediency appear, in liberal morality, to override reasons of principle so much more readily in public than in private life?"[35] The question is posed as though the issue were this: why might Churchill be obliged to allow Coventry to be bombed without warning its inhabitants of impending attack, as Prime Minister, while, as a man, such an omission would be completely inexcusable? Churchill as Prime Minister provides us with his hands. When he acts, we are, as Hobbes described it, the author of his acts and he acts with our authority. The complexity of the moral relationship between institutions, decision makers, and those they represent means that if a political leader acts on our behalf and with a mandate we provided, if he or she acts as our representative, and in circumstances and through institutions that explicitly call for or are constituted by that leader's agency, is only the leader accountable , or is there filth on our hands also? And if the latter, how might this affect the design of institutions of accountability? If our representatives act on our behalf, can they be punished on our behalf also? These pressing questions, empirical and philosophical, remain to be addressed.

Emergency exists at the intersection of law, morality, and politics. We have seen that a focus on any of these to the exclusion of the others yields a lopsided picture with dangerous results. The rule of law alone cannot make us safe. Nor can the pure deductive ethics of philosophical liberalism. For, the identification of "morality with innocence ... would ultimately set the politicians free to disregard morality altogether."[36]

---

[35] Benn, "Private and Public Morality," p. 163.
[36] Hampshire, *Innocence and Experience*, p. 12.

We do not deduce the application of the law from the law and the general case. We do not deduce the moral course of action from the moral law and the general case. Agency figures also. We must confront and embrace the exceptionalist insight that the law never rules on its own, that agency forms a central part of institutions. But we must resist the temptation to eschew law entirely when law becomes inconvenient. Instead, we look to the ends of the state and employ means most conducive to those ends, in the light of principles that bound the edges.

Our commitment to liberal democratic values can and has survived periods of emergency. From a pragmatic perspective, the arguments I have made offer hope that further empirical and normative scholarship might give liberal democracies assistance to better navigate the rocks and shoals of power concentration and rights derogation in the future. But we have seen that engagement with emergency holds lessons of a more profound character also. Emergency is one manifestation of tensions between order and justice, and between constraint and enablement of power, and it demonstrates vividly the dangers of an innocent engagement with politics.

Bibliography

Ackerman, Bruce. *Before the Next Attack: Preserving Civil Liberties in an Age of Terrorism*. New Haven: Yale University Press, 2006.

———. "The Emergency Constitution," *Yale Law Journal*, vol. 113, 2004, pp. 1029–91.

Agamben, Giorgio. *State of Exception*. Trans. Kevin Attell. Chicago: University of Chicago Press, 2005.

Arendt, Hannah. *The Origins of Totalitarianism*. San Diego: Harcourt Press, 1968.

Aristotle. *Nichomachean Ethics*. Trans. J. A. K. Thomson. London: Penguin, 2004.

———. *The Politics*. Trans. Carnes Lord. Chicago: University of Chicago Press, 1984.

Baehr, Peter, and Melvin Richter (eds.). *Dictatorship in History and Theory*. Cambridge: Cambridge University Press, 2004.

Beiner, Ronald. *Political Judgment*. London: Methuen, 1983.

Benn, Stanley I. "Private and Public Morality: Clean Living and Dirty Hands." In S. I. Benn and G. F. Gaus (eds.), *Public and Private in Social Life*, London: Croom Helm, 1983, pp. 155–81.

Berlin, Isaiah. *The Crooked Timber of Humanity: Chapters in the History of Ideas*, Princeton: Princeton University Press, 1990.

———. "The Originality of Machiavelli." In Henry Hardy (ed.), *Against the Current: Essays in the History of Ideas*, Oxford: Clarendon Press, 1980, pp. 25–79.

Brandt, R. B. "Utilitarianism and the Rules of War," *Philosophy and Public Affairs*, vol. 1, no. 2, 1971–72, pp. 145–65.

Caldwell, P. *The Theory and Practice of Weimar Constitutionalism*. Durham, NC: Duke University Press, 1997.

Chesterman, Simon. "Deny Everything: Intelligence Activities and the Rule of Law." In Victor V. Ramraj (ed.), *Emergencies and the Limits of Legality*, Cambridge: Cambridge University Press, 2008, pp. 313–33.

Cicero. *The Republic and the Laws*. Trans. Niall Rudd. Oxford: Oxford University Press, 1998.

D'Amato, Anthony. "Legal and Moral Dimensions of Churchill's Failure to Warn," *Cardozo Law Review*, vol. 20, 1998, pp. 561–7.

de Maistre, Joseph. *Considerations on France*. Cambridge: Cambridge University Press, 1994.

———. *The Works of Joseph de Maistre*. Ed. Jack Lively. London: George Allen & Unwin, 1965.

Dennison, George M. "Martial Law: The Development of a Theory of Emergency Powers, 1776–1861," *American Journal of Legal History*, vol. 18, no. 1, January 1974 pp. 52–79.

Derbyshire, J. Denis, and Ian Derbyshire. *Political Systems of the World*. Edinburgh: Chambers, 1989.

Dhar, P. N. *Indira Gandhi, the "Emergency," and Indian Democracy*. New York: Oxford University Press, 2000.

Dicey, A.V. *Introduction to the Study of the Law of the Constitution*. London: Macmillan, 1915.

Dietz, Mary. "Trapping the Prince: Machiavelli and the Politics of Deception," *American Political Science Review*, vol. 80, no. 3, September, 1986, pp. 777–99.

Dionysius. *The Roman Antiquities*. Trans. Earnest Cary. Cambridge, MA: Harvard University Press, 1940.

Donagan, Alan. *The Theory of Morality*. Chicago: University of Chicago Press, 1977.

Donohue, Laura. *Counter-Terrorist Law and Emergency Power in the United Kingdom 1922–2000*. Dublin: Irish Academic Press, 2001.

Dunn, John. *Locke*. Oxford: Oxford University Press, 1984.

———. *The Political Thought of John Locke*. Cambridge: Cambridge University Press, 1969.

Dworkin, Ronald. *Taking Rights Seriously*. Cambridge, MA: Harvard University Press, 1977.

———. "Terror and the Attack on Civil Liberties," *New York Review of Books*, vol. 50, no. 17, November 6 2003.

Dyzenhaus, David. *The Constitution of Law: Legality in a Time of Emergency*. Cambridge: Cambridge University Press, 2006.

———. *Legality and Legitimacy: Carl Schmitt, Hans Kelsen, and Hermann Heller in Weimar*. Oxford: Clarendon Press, 1997.

Egyptian Organization for Human Rights. *The Effect of the Emergency Law on the Human Rights Situation in Egypt: 1992–2002*. http://www.eohr.org/report/2003/emergency.HTM. Accessed 10/2004.

Epstein, Lee, Daniel Ho, Gary King, and Jeffrey A. Segal. "The Supreme Court during Crisis," *New York University Law Review*, vol. 80, 2005, pp. 1–116.

Etzioni, Amitai (ed.). *Rights vs. Public Safety after September 11*. Lanham, MD: Rowman & Littlefield, 2003.

Fairman, Charles. *The Law of Martial Rule*. 2nd edn. Chicago: Callaghan and Company, 1943.

Fallon, Richard. "'The Rule of Law' as a Concept in Constitutional Discourse," *Columbia Law Review*, vol. 97, 1997, pp. 1–56.

Fatovic, Clement. "Constitutionalism and Contingency: Locke's Theory of Prerogative," *History of Political Thought*, vol. 25, 2004, pp. 276–97.

———. "Constitutionalism and Presidential Prerogative: Jeffersonian and Hamiltonian Perspectives," *American Journal of Political Science*, vol. 48, July 2004, pp. 429–44.

Ferejohn, John, and Pasquale Pasquino. "The Law of Exception: A Typology of Emergency Powers," *International Journal of Constitutional Law*, vol. 2, April 2004, pp. 210–39.

Finalson, W. F. *Review of the Authorities as the Repression of Riot or Rebellion with Special Reference to Criminal or Civil Liability*. London: Stevens and Richardson, 1868.

Flanz, Gisbert H. (ed.). *Constitutions of the Countries of the World*. Dobbs Ferry, NY: Oceana Publications, 2003.

Fogarty, Kenneth. *Equality Rights and Their Limitation in the Charter*. Toronto: Carswell, 1987.

Foucault, Michel. *Discipline and Punish*. 2nd edn. Trans. Alan Sheridan. New York: Random House, 1995.

Franklin, Daniel. *Extraordinary Measures: The Exercise of Prerogative Powers in the United States*. Pittsburgh: University of Pittsburgh Press, 1991.

Friederich, C. J. *Constitutional Reason of State*. Providence: Brown University Press, 1957.

Galston, William A. "What Is Living and What Is Dead in Kant's Practical Philosophy?" In R. Beiner and W. Booth (eds.), *Kant and Political Philosophy*, New Haven: Yale University Press, 1993, pp. 207–23.

Gardiner, S.R. *The Personal Government of Charles I: 1628–1642*. London: Longmans and Green, 1877.

Garner, Anthony. "Martial Law, Military Government and the Writ of Habeas Corpus in Hawaii," *California Law Review*, vol. 31, 1943, pp. 477–514.

Green, Leslie. "Internal Minorities and Their Rights." In J. Baker (ed.), *Group Rights*, Toronto: University of Toronto Press, 1994, pp. 100–17.

Gregor, Mary. *Laws of Freedom. A Study of Kant's Method of Applying the Categorical Imperative in the Metaphysik der Sitten*. New York: Barnes and Noble, 1963.

Gross, Oren. "The Concept of 'Crisis': What Can We Learn from the Two Dictatorships of L. Quinctius Cincinnatus?," *Diritti Civili ed Economici in Tempi di Crisi*, vol. 21, 2006.

———. "Providing for the Unexpected: Constitutional Emergency Provisions," *Israel Yearbook on Human Rights*, vol. 33, 2003, p. 13ff.

————, and Fionnuala Ní Aoláin. *Law in Times of Crisis: Emergency Powers in Theory and Practice*. Cambridge: Cambridge University Press, 2006.

Gupte, Pranay. *Mother India: A Political Biography of Indira Gandhi*. New York: Scribner's, 1992.

Hale, Matthew. *The History of the Common Law of England*. Ed. Charles M. Gray. Chicago: University of Chicago Press, 1971.

Hamilton, Alexander, James Madison, and John Jay. *The Federalist*. New York: Penguin, 1961.

Hampshire, Stuart. *Innocence and Experience*. Cambridge, MA: Harvard University Press, 1989.

———— (ed.). *Public and Private Morality*. Cambridge: Cambridge University Press, 1978.

Hare, R. M. "Rules of War and Moral Reasoning," *Philosophy and Public Affairs*, vol. 1, 1971–72, pp. 166–81.

Hart, James. "The Emergency Ordinance: A Note on Executive Power," *Columbia Law Review*, vol. 23, June 1923, pp. 528–35.

Hartfield, Marriane Elizabeth. "The Roman Dictatorship: Its Character and Its Evolution." Doctoral Dissertation. University of California, Berkeley, 1982.

Hassner, Pierre. "Immanuel Kant," *History of Political Philosophy*. 3rd edn. Ed. Leo Strauss and Joseph Cropsey. Chicago: University of Chicago Press, 1987, pp.581–621.

Hatchard, John. *Individual Freedoms and State Security in the African Context*. Harare: Baobab Books, 1993.

————. "States of Siege/Emergency in Africa," *Journal of African Law*, vol. 37, 1993, pp. 104–8.

Hayek, F. W. *The Constitution of Liberty*. Chicago: University of Chicago Press, 1960.

Heymann, B. *Terrorism, Freedom, and Security: Winning without War*. Cambridge, MA: MIT Press, 2003.

Hiebert, Janet L. *Limiting Rights*. Montreal and Kingston: McGill-Queens University Press, 1996.

Hill, Thomas E. Jr., "Making Exceptions without Abandoning the Principle: or How a Kantian Might Think about Terrorism." In R. G. Frey and Christopher Morris (eds.), *Violence, Terrorism, and Justice*, Cambridge: Cambridge University Press, 1991, pp. 196–229.

Hinsley, F. H. *British Intelligence in the Second World War*. London: HMSO, 1993.

Hobbes, Thomas. *Leviathan*. Oxford: Clarendon Press, 1909.

Holdsworth, W. S. "Martial Law Historically Considered," *Law Quarterly Review*, vol. 117, 1902, pp. 117–32.

Hollis, Martin. "Dirty Hands," *British Journal of Political Science*, vol. 12, October 1982, pp. 385–98.

Holmes, Stephen, and Cass Sunstein. *The Cost of Rights*. New York: Norton, 1999.

Hulliung, Mark. *Citizen Machiavelli*. Princeton, Princeton University Press, 1983.

Hulugalle, H. A. J. *British Governors of Ceylon*. Colombo: Associated Newspapers of Ceylon, 1963.

Hussain, Nasser. *The Jurisprudence of Emergency*. Ann Arbor: University of Michigan, 2003.

Ignatieff, Michael. *The Lesser Evil: Political Ethics in an Age of Terror*. Princeton: Princeton University Press, 2004.

International Commission of Jurists. *States of Emergency: Their Impact on Human Rights*. Geneva: 1983.

Iyer, Venkat. *States of Emergency: The Indian Experience*. New Dehli: Butterworths, 2000.

Jeffery, Keith, and Peter Hennessy. *States of Emergency: British Governments and Strikebreaking since 1919*. London: Routledge and Kegan Paul, 1983.

Jolley, Nicholas. *Locke: His Philosophical Thought*. Oxford: Oxford University Press, 1999.

Kaes, Anton, Martin Jay, and Edward Dimendberg (eds.). *The Weimar Republic Sourcebook*. Berkeley: University of California Press, 1994.

Kant, Immanuel. *Critique of Pure Reason*. Trans. Norman Kemp Smith. New York: St. Martin's Press, 1929.

———. *Groundwork for the Metaphysics of Morals*. Trans. James W. Ellington. Indianapolis: Hackett, 1981.

———. *Kant's Political Writings*. 2nd edn. Ed. Hans Reiss. Cambridge: Cambridge University Press, 1991.

———. *The Metaphysics of Morals*. Trans. Mary Gregor. Cambridge: Cambridge University Press, 1991.

Kelsen, Hans. *General Theory of Norms*. Vol. 1. Trans. Michael Hartney. Oxford: Clarendon Press, 1991.

Kraynack, Robert P. "Hobbes' Behemoth and the Argument for Absolutism," *American Political Science Review*, vol. 76, December 1982, pp. 837–47.

Kymlicka, Will. *Liberalism, Community, and Culture*. Oxford: Clarendon Press, 1989.

———. *Multicultural Citizenship*. Oxford: Oxford University Press, 1985.

Larmore, Charles. *Patterns of Moral Complexity*. Cambridge: Cambridge University Press, 1987.

Lazar, Nomi Claire. "The Scope of Liberalism: The Implications of the Ethico-Political Status of Ethnic Minorities for the Relationship of Liberal Theory to Political Morality." MA Dissertation, University of London, 1999.

———. "A Topography of Emergency Powers." In Victor V. Ramraj (ed.), *Emergencies and the Limits of Legality*, Cambridge: Cambridge University Press, 2008, pp. 156–71.

Lillich, Robert. "The Paris Minimum Standards of Human Rights Norms in a State of Emergency," *American Journal of International Law*, vol. 79, 1985, pp. 1072–81.

Lintott, Andrew. *The Constitution of the Roman Republic.* Oxford: Oxford University Press, 1999.

Livy. *The History of Rome since Its Foundation.* Vols. 1 and 2. Trans. Aubrey de Selincourt. London: Penguin, 2002.

———. *The War with Hannibal.* Trans. Aubrey de Selincourt. London: Penguin, 1986.

Lobel, Jules. "Emergency Power and the Decline of Liberalism," *Yale Law Journal,* vol. 98, May 1989, pp. 1385–433.

Locke, John. *Educational Writings of John Locke.* Ed. James L. Axtell. Cambridge: Cambridge University Press, 1968.

———. *An Essay Concerning Human Understanding.* Oxford: Clarendon Press, 1926.

———. *A Letter Concerning Toleration.* Indianapolis: Hackett, 1983.

———. *Second Treatise of Government.* New York: Liberal Arts Press, 1952.

Ludowyk, E. F. C. *The Modern History of Ceylon.* London: Weidenfeld and Nicolson, 1966.

Machiavelli, Niccoló. *The Prince and Discourses.* Trans. Luigi Ricci and E. R. P. Vincent. New York: Random House, 1950.

Maguire, John. "Internment, the IRA, and the Lawless Case in Ireland, 1957–61," *Journal of the Oxford University Historical Society,* Fall 2004.

Manitoba Water Commission. *An Independent Review of Actions Taken during the 1997 Red River Flood: Report to the Hon. J. Glen Cummings Minister of Natural Resources.* Winnepeg: Manitoba Water Commission, June 1998.

Mansfield, Harvey. *Taming the Prince.* New York: Free Press, 1989.

Marcus, Ruth. "Moral Dilemmas and Consistency," *Journal of Philosophy,* vol. 77, March 1980, pp. 121–36.

McCormick, John P. *Carl Schmitt's Critique of Liberalism.* Cambridge: Cambridge University Press, 1997.

———. "Contain the Wealthy and Patrol the Magistrates: Restoring Elite Accountability to Popular Government," *American Political Science Review,* May 2006, pp. 147–63.

Medina, Vicente. "Locke's Militant Liberalism," *History of Philosophy Quarterly,* vol. 19, October 2002, pp. 345–65.

Meinecke, Friederich. *Machiavellism: The Doctrine of Raison D'état and Its Place in Modern History.* Trans. Douglas Scott. New Haven: Yale University Press, 1957.

Mill, John Stuart. *Utilitarianism.* London: J. M. Dent, 1910.

Millgram, Elijah (ed.). *Varieties of Practical Reasoning.* Cambridge, MA: MIT Press, 2001.

Minattur, Joseph. *Martial Law in India, Pakistan, and Ceylon.* The Hague: Martinus Nijhoff, 1962.

Neumann, Franz. "The Concept of Political Freedom," *Columbia Law Review,* vol. 53, November 1953.

Nichols, Ray. "Maxims, 'Practical Wisdom' and the Language of Action: Beyond Grand Theory," *Political Theory*, vol. 24, November 1996, pp. 687–705.

Nicolet, Claude. "Le Dictature à Rome." In Maurice Duverger (ed.), *Dictature et Légitimité*, Paris: Presses universitaires de France, 1982.

Nozick, Robert. *Anarchy, State, and Utopia*. New York: Basic Books, 1974.

Oraà, Jaime. *Human Rights in States of Emergency in International Law*. Oxford: Clarendon Press, 1992.

Özbudun, Ergun, and Mehmet Turhan. *Emergency Powers*. Strasbourg: Council of Europe Publishing, 1995.

Park, Richard L. "Political Crisis in India," *Asian Survey*, vol. 15, no. 11, 1975, pp. 996–1013.

Pasquino, Pasquale. "Locke on King's Prerogative," *Political Theory*, vol. 26, no. 2, 1998, pp. 198–208.

Paton, H. J. *The Categorical Imperative: A Study in Kant's Moral Theory*. Philadelphia: University of Pennsylvania Press, 1971.

Phillimore, G. G. "Martial Law in Rebellion," *Journal of the Society of Comparative Legislation*, vol. 2, no. 1, 1900, pp. 45–72.

Pitkin, Hannah. *Fortune Is a Woman*. Berkeley: University of California Press, 1984.

Pocock, J. G. A. *The Machiavellian Moment: Florentine Political Thought and the Atlantic Republican Tradition*. Princeton: Princeton University Press, 1975.

Posner, Eric A., and Adrian, Vermeule. "Emergencies and Democratic Failure," *Virginia Law Review*, vol. 96, no. 2, pp. 1091–146.

Posner, Richard. *Not a Suicide Pact*. Oxford: Oxford University Press, 2006.

Radin, M. "Martial Law and the State of Siege," *California Law Review*, vol. 30, 1942, p. 634ff.

Ramraj, Victor V. (ed.). *Emergencies and the Limits of Legality*. Cambridge: Cambridge University Press, 2008.

Rawls, John. *The Law of Peoples*. Cambridge, MA: Harvard University Press, 1999.

———. *Political Liberalism*. New York: Columbia University Press, 1993.

———. *A Theory of Justice*. Cambridge, MA: Belknap Press, 1971.

Raz, Joseph. *The Morality of Freedom*. Oxford: Clarendon, 1986.

Rehnquist, William H. *All the Laws but One*. New York: Random House, 1998.

Roach, Kent. *September 11: Consequences for Canada*. Montreal: McGill-Queen's University Press, 2003.

Rommen, Heinrich A. *The Natural Law: A Study in Legal and Social History and Philosophy*. Trans. Thomas R. Hanley. St. Louis: B. Herder Book Co., 1947.

Rosas, Allan. "Emergency Regimes: A Comparison." In Donna Gomien (ed.), *Broadening Frontiers of Human Rights*, Oslo: Scandinavian University Press, 1993.

Rosen, Allen D. *Kant's Theory of Justice*. Ithaca: Cornell Press, 1993.

Rossiter, Clinton. *Constitutional Dictatorship*. 2nd edn. New Brunswick: Transaction Press, 2002.

Rousseau, Jean-Jacques. *Du contrat social*. Paris: Flammarion, 1992.

———. *Discours sur l'origine et les fondements de l'inégalité parmi les hommes*. Paris: Flammarion, 1971.

———. *Émile*. Trans. Allan Bloom. New York: Basic Books, 1979.

———. *The Government of Poland*. Trans. Willmoore Kendall. Indianapolis: Hackett Publishing, 1985.

Rynard, Paul, and David P. Shugarman (eds.). *Cruelty and Deception*. Peterborough, OR: Broadview Press, 2000.

Sartre, Jean-Paul. *Les mains sales*. Paris: Librairie Gallimard, 1948.

Scheiber, Harry N., and Jane L. Scheiber. "Bayonets in Paradise: A Half-Century Retrospect on Martial Law in Hawai'i, 1941–1946," *Hawai'i Law Review*, vol. 19, 1997, pp. 477–648.

Scheppele, Kim Lane. *The International State of Emergency*, http://digitalcommons.law.umaryland.edu/schmooze_papers/49, accessed 2006.

———. "Law in a Time of Emergency," *University of Pennsylvania Journal of Constitutional Law*, vol. 6, 2004, pp. 1001–83.

———. "Small Emergencies," *Georgia Law Review*, vol. 40, pp. 835–62.

Scheuerman, William. "Rethinking Crisis Government," *Constellations*, vol. 9, no. 4, 2002, pp. 492–505.

Schmitt, Carl. *The Concept of the Political*. Trans. George Schwab. New Brunswick, NJ: Rutgers University Press, 1976.

———. *The Crisis of Parliamentary Democracy*. Trans. Ellen Kennedy. Cambridge, MA: MIT Press, 1985.

———. *Die Diktatur*. 6th edn. Berlin: Duncker & Humblot, 1994.

———. *The Leviathan in the State Theory of Thomas Hobbes: Meaning and Failure of a Political Symbol*. Trans. George Schwab and Erna Hilfstein. Westport: Greenwood Press, 1996.

———. *Political Theology*. Trans. George Schwab. Cambridge, MA: MIT Press, 1985.

Schreurer, Christoph. "Derogation of Human Rights in Situations of Public Emergency: The Experience of the European Convention on Human Rights," *Yale Journal of World Public Order*, vol. 9, no. 1, 1982, pp. 113–32.

Shapiro, Ian. *The Evolution of Rights in Liberal Theory*. Cambridge: Cambridge University Press, 1982.

———. *The Flight from Reality in the Social Sciences*. Princeton: Princeton University Press, 2005.

——— (ed.). *The Rule of Law*. New York: New York University Press, 1994.

———. *The State of Democratic Theory*. Princeton: Princeton University Press, 2003.

Sharpe, R. J. *The Law of Habeas Corpus*. Oxford: Clarendon Press, 1989.

Shklar, Judith. *Men and Citizens*. Cambridge, MA: Harvard University Press, 1969.

Shwayder, D. S. "Moral Maxims and Moral Rules," *Ethics*, vol. 67, July 1957, pp. 269–85.

Smith, Steven B. "Hegel's Views on War, the State, and International Relations," *American Political Science Review*, vol. 77, September 1983. pp. 624–32.

Sofaer, Abraham. "Emergency Powers and the Hero of New Orleans," *Cardozo Law Review*, vol. 2, no. 2, 1981, pp. 233–53.

Sorrel, Tom (ed.). *The Cambridge Companion to Hobbes*. Cambridge: Cambridge University Press, 1996.

Stavros, Stephanos. "The Right to a Fair Trial in Emergency Situations," *International and Comparative Law Quarterly*, vol. 41, April 1992, pp. 343–65.

Stephen, James Fitzjames. *A History of the Criminal Law of England*. London: Macmillan, 1993.

Strauss, Leo. *Natural Right and History*. Chicago: University of Chicago Press, 1965.

———. "Notes on Carl Schmitt, the Concept of the Political," In *Concept of the Political*. Trans. Harvey J. Lomax. Chicago: University of Chicago Press, 1996, pp. 83–107.

———. *Thoughts on Machiavelli*. Chicago: University of Chicago Press, 1958.

Sullivan, Vicki. "Machiavelli's Momentary 'Machiavellian Moment': A Reconsideration of Pocock's Treatment of the Discourses," *Political Theory*, vol. 20, May 1992, pp. 309–18.

Svensson-McCarthy, Anna-Lena. *International Law of Human Rights and States of Exception*. The Hague: Martinus Nijhoff Publishers, 1998.

Tamir, Yael. *Liberal Nationalism*. Princeton: Princeton University Press, 1993.

United Nations Commission on Human Rights. *Concluding Observations of the Committee Against Torture*, Egypt 17/05/99, A/54/44.

———. *Concluding Observations of the Human Rights Committee*, Egypt 09/08/93, CCPR/C/79/Add.23.

———. *Eighth Annual Report and List of States which, since 1 January 1985 Have Proclaimed, Extended, or Terminated a State of Emergency*. 26 June 1995, Document E/CN.4/Sub.2/1995/20*.

Walzer, Michael. *Just and Unjust Wars*. London: Penguin Books, 1977.

———. "Political Action and the Problem of Dirty Hands," *Philosophy and Public Affairs*, vol. 2, 1973, pp. 160–80.

Weber, Max. "Politics as a Vocation." In H. H. Gerth and C. Wright Mills (eds.), *From Max Weber*. New York: Oxford University Press, 1946, pp. 77–128.

White, Robert W., and Terry Falkenberg White. "Repression and the Liberal State: The Case of Northern Ireland 1969–1972," *Journal of Conflict Resolution*, vol. 39, June 1995, pp. 330–52.

Wolff, Hans Julius. *Roman Law: An Historical Introduction*. Norman, OK: University of Oklahoma Press, 1951.

Wolin, Sheldon. *Politics and Vision*. Boston: Little, Brown, 1960.

Wood, Allen W. *Kant's Ethical Thought*. Cambridge: Cambridge University Press, 1999.

Wood, Diane P. "The Rule of Law in Times of Stress," *University of Chicago Law Review*, vol. 70, 2003, pp. 455–70.

Zuckert, Michael P. *Natural Rights and the New Republicanism*. Princeton: Princeton University Press, 1994.

Index